Law in Everyday Life

John Seely

Cartoons by Beatrice Baumgartner-Cohen

OXFORD UNIVERSITY PRESS

Great Clarendon Street, Oxford OX2 6DP

Oxford University Press is a department of the University of Oxford.
It furthers the University's objective of excellence in research, scholarship,
and education by publishing worldwide in
Oxford New York
Auckland Bangkok Buenos Aires Cape Town Chennai
Dar es Salaam Delhi Hong Kong Istanbul Karachi Kolkata
Kuala Lumpur Madrid Melbourne Mexico City Mumbai Nairobi
São Paulo Shanghai Taipei Tokyo Toronto

Published in the United States
by Oxford University Press Inc., New York

First published 2003

British Library Cataloguing in Publication Data
Data available

Library of Congress Cataloging in Publication Data
Data available

ISBN 0-19-860674-5

10 9 8 7 6 5 4 3 2 1

Typeset by Footnote Graphics Ltd, Warminster, Wiltshire
Printed by Giunti Industrie Grafiche, Prato, Italy

La

Joh
exp
con
har
Edi

One Step Ahead . . .

The *One Step Ahead* series is for all those who want and need to communicate more effectively in a range of real-life situations. Each title provides up-to-date practical guidance, tips, and the language tools to enhance your writing and speaking.

Series Editor: John Seely

Titles in the series

CVs and Job Applications*	Judith Leigh
Editing and Revising Text	Jo Billingham
Essays and Dissertations	Chris Mounsey
Giving Presentations	Jo Billingham
Law in Everyday Life	John Seely
Organizing and Participating in Meetings	Judith Leigh
Presenting Numbers, Tables, and Charts	Sally Bigwood and Melissa Spore
Publicity, Newsletters, and Press Releases	Alison Baverstock
Punctuation	Robert Allen
Spelling	Robert Allen
Words	John Seely
Writing Bids and Funding Applications*	Jane Dorner
Writing for the Internet	Jane Dorner
Writing Reports	John Seely

**forthcoming*

Acknowledgements

I am grateful to the following for help with particular aspects of the law: Louisa Cross of The Solicitors' Family Law Association; Jane Keir, Head of Department of Family Law, Kingsley Napley Solicitors; and Detective Sergeant Ben Snuggs, Hampshire Constabulary. I should also like to thank the readers who commented on the text in an earlier draft and Alysoun Owen of Oxford University Press for her comments and encouragement. Needless to say, while I have taken careful note of comments and criticism, responsibility for the text is mine alone.

The publisher and author are grateful to the Community Legal Service for permission to use the screenshot from their web site 'JustAsk' on page 7.

Contents

1 Introduction

The law seems to permeate every aspect of our lives. As I write the opening paragraph of this book, I am carrying out my part of a legal contract with the publisher which runs to over 5,000 words. And what words! For example:

> 5.1.1 the Author hereby grants to the Publisher during the legal term of copyright including any renewals and extensions thereof an exclusive licence on the terms and conditions herein contained to produce or publish the work . . .

Popular perceptions of law and lawyers are that:

- The law is unnecessarily complicated. It uses long incomprehensible sentences stuffed with jargon.
- Lawyers speak this language to each other so as to exclude the rest of us.
- When we have to consult them, lawyers charge an inordinate amount of money.

Some of this is undoubtedly true. It takes years of training to qualify as a solicitor and even longer to make a success as a barrister. Those who succeed can perhaps be forgiven if they aim to make all those years pay off. And they can point to the disasters that occur when laypeople try to approach the law on a D-I-Y basis.

But painting the portrait of law and lawyers in this negative way is misleading. It is true that the volume of legislation and regulation increases every year, but there are those in the profession and outside it who are working hard and with some success to make the law clearer and more accessible to those it is meant to serve. For example, if you have to make a small claim (up to £5,000) against someone who owes you money, there is a special and simplified procedure that enables you to do so. And those whose first serious encounter with the courts is a divorce case will find that the language and approach adopted are much more practical and humane than was the case even twenty years ago. In this age of electronic information, the legal system has used the new technology to explain itself to the general public in a number of web sites that offer clear, straightforward information and advice:

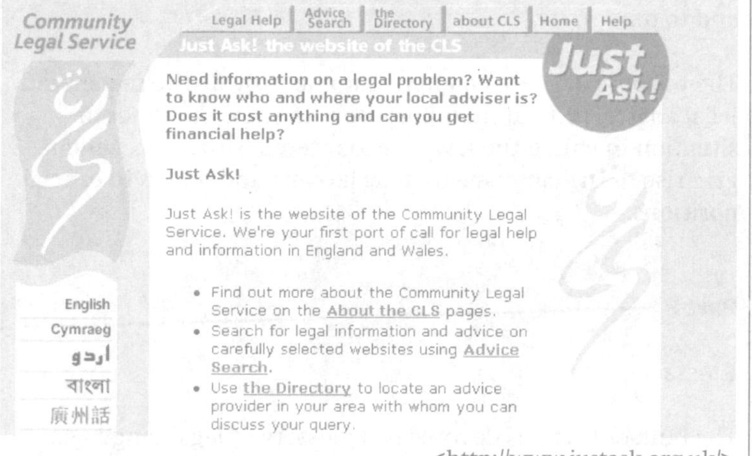

<http://www.justask.org.uk/>

The **Community Legal Service** is a government service which provides guidance on where to get legal advice and how to apply for legal aid. It also publishes a range of advisory leaflets.

This book is written from the perspective of a 'customer' of the law. In my own life I encounter the law as a private individual, as a self-employed writer, and as a member of the Boards of two small companies, both of which frequently take advice from lawyers. I also bring to the writing a deep interest in language and communication. The law referred to throughout is that of England and Wales; Scotland has its own legal system, which is significantly different.

In the writing of this book I have received help and guidance from a number of lawyers, some of whom are listed in the Acknowledgments on page 2. I am very grateful to them for their patience and encouragement. Needless to say, the opinions expressed throughout are my own.

How the book works

Like others in the *One Step Ahead* series, this book is in two main parts.

Part A

Chapter topics
2 Important concepts
3 The legal system
4 From cradle to grave
5 The law and the householder
6 The law and the driver
7 The world of work
8 Money and shopping
9 Human rights

The first part provides a brief and simple description of the main areas of everyday life in which ordinary people encounter the law. Chapter 2 explains some key concepts, while Chapter 3 gives an overview of the legal system. Chapters 4 to 9 look at particular situations and areas of life: employment, driving, and so on.

The purpose of these chapters is not to provide the reader with legal advice. Instead their purpose is to show the kinds of situation in which the law is encountered, situations which give rise to the language used by lawyers and others in official positions.

Part B

Glossary

The bulk of Part B is devoted to a glossary of legal language. Words and concepts are explained and there are cross-references to the relevant pages in Part A.

Resources

There is also a Resources section. Here you will find listed organizations, books, and web sites where more detailed information and advice can be found.

m.p.h. in a built-up area? Never? Have you never been guilty of careless driving? If you were tried and found guilty of either offence you would have committed a crime, as surely as if you went up to your local jeweller's and put a brick through the window in order to steal expensive watches.

But most of us don't look at it in this way. A few m.p.h. over the speed limit, a slightly dodgy bit of overtaking—they don't really feel like crimes, do they? But they are. Motoringof fences are tried in exactly the same way as other crimes, and those who are found guilty can be fined thousands of pounds, or sentenced to imprisonment, just as any other criminal. Motoring offences are different, however, in one important respect. A person accused of other crimes has to be shown to have *intended* to commit the act. For example, if you are caught shoplifting it is a reasonable defence to say that you intended to pay for the item but forgot; that you didn't intend to commit an offence. (It may well not work, of course.) No such defence is possible if you are caught speeding. In the case of motoring offences, it is sufficient for the prosecution to prove that you

strict liability
In criminal law this means offences where the prosecution do not have to show *mens rea* (guilty intent). Motoring offences such as speeding come into this category.

Magistrates' Court the lowest level of court in which cases are heard by *magistrates*.

See chapter 4 page 41

maintenance order an order made by a court for a parent to contribute financially towards the support of a spouse or child. Orders for the support of children are now normally handled by the *Child Support Agency*.

See chapter 2 page 13

malice aforethought a key part of the definition of *murder*; the *mens rea* for this crime. Confusingly, it does not necessarily mean that the offender felt malice towards the victim nor that the crime was planned in advance. It means that at the time the act was committed the offender either intended to kill the victim or to cause them grievous bodily harm and that death was the result.

www.family-solicitors.co.uk
A site providing access to local solicitors dealing with family matters plus guidance screens on a range of topics from adoption to wills.

www.justask.org.uk
Web site of the Community Legal Service, the government service offering guidance on where to get legal advice and the source of legal aid in civil cases. It offers a number of useful leaflets produced by the Consumers' Association on topics such as divorce, making a will, employment law, renting and letting property, and buying and selling a house.

2 Important concepts

CONTENTS

This chapter is about some of the ideas behind our legal system. If you sometimes wonder why the elaborate structure of our law is so complicated, or exactly what concepts like 'tort' mean, then this chapter is for you. If such things seem academic and remote, then you may prefer to skip to the later chapters dealing with specific aspects of the law. All the legal terms used in this chapter can also be found in the Glossary.

What is the law?

The law exists to ensure that civilized life is possible:

There is more about criminal law in this chapter on pages 12-13 and in chapter 9 on pages 88-91.

- **Compulsion**
  The law ensures that individual citizens can go about their daily business without being attacked or robbed, and that society can set up institutions which will be respected by the individual. To do this, the government provides the legal machine with the weapons of compulsion: police to enforce the law and catch those who break it, courts to establish guilt and innocence, and prisons to punish offenders.

An important aspect of constitutional law concerns civil liberties. This is covered in chapter 9.

- **The Constitution**
  Government itself is defined by constitutional laws. In Britain some of the most fundamental laws of our constitution are traditional rather than being written down, but there is also a mass of written law covering how we are governed, both centrally and by local authorities.

- **A framework**
  As individuals we want to be able to make private arrangements between ourselves, secure in the knowledge that if others break their word, we will be compensated for

our loss. We want to make sure that other people cannot spoil our enjoyment of our property or hurt us physically by their carelessness—and that if they do we can get them to stop and/or be compensated. The law provides a framework within which we can protect ourselves in this way.

- **A system**
  To achieve all these things we need a law that is consistent and consistently applied. So we need a legal system that is capable of applying the law fairly and consistently and amending and interpreting it so that it can deal with new and changing circumstances.

The legal system of England and Wales is described in chapter 3.

Public and private law

So we need law that deals with the whole of society, but which also serves us as individuals.

The good of the people is the first law.

Cicero, *Roman statesman, lawyer, orator, and author*

Public law is those branches of the law that deal with society as a whole and the individual citizen's relationship with society.

- criminal law
- constitutional law
- tax law
- administrative law
  (All the rules and regulations set up by government departments in areas such as social security.)

Private law covers relationships between individuals, groups, and organizations:

- family law
- company law
- contract law
- the law of tort.

Some aspects of family law are covered in chapter 4. There is more about contract law and the law of tort later in this chapter.

Crime

Being a thief is a terrific life, but the trouble is they put you in the nick for it.

John McVicar, *former convict*

People want to live in an orderly society in which they can go about their public and private lives without fear of being injured or having their property damaged or stolen by others. We wish to be free to do as we like without harming others and without interference from others. We also allow the state to stop us from doing things that harm ourselves. In addition we empower the state to protect us from threats from outside the country and to protect our security. Individual citizens have to be prevented from acting in a way that threatens national security. In order to achieve this we empower the state to pass and enforce laws and to punish those who break them. This is the foundation on which the criminal law is built: to prevent individuals from behaving in ways which harm others or society as a whole.

Criminal law protects...

- **the state against individuals**
  This is the basis of laws about national security.
- **the individual from harm by others**
  By, for example, laws about murder, assault, and rape, as well as lesser offences such as careless driving.
- **the individual's property**
- **the individual from his own unwise actions, which may also harm others**
  This is why there are laws banning drugs and laws against obscenity.

How do we define a crime?

Lawyers use two Latin phrases when they are defining crimes: *actus reus* and *mens rea. Actus reus* means literally 'guilty act'. To find someone guilty of a crime it has to be proved that they committed an action defined by the law as a crime. So, for example, the law distinguishes between the crimes of assault and battery. Assault means acting in such a way towards someone that they are put in fear of personal injury. In other words you can assault someone without touching them. Battery, on the other hand, means deliberately making physical contact with someone without their consent.

Crime is a logical extension of the sort of behaviour that is often considered perfectly respectable in legitimate business.

Robert Rice, *American author*

The last sentence contained the word 'deliberately'. *Mens rea* is the second component of a crime and means 'guilty mind'. A crime is a criminal act done with a 'guilty mind'. The law distinguishes different degrees in this. For some crimes, like murder, it has to be proved that there was specific intent: when X raised the axe he specifically intended to kill Y. For other crimes, it is necessary to prove recklessness or negligence by the perpetrator. There is a fourth group of crimes in which the perpetrator's state of mind is of no importance. If you are caught by a police speed trap breaking the speed limit it makes no difference at all whether you intended to or not; the simple fact of exceeding the limit is sufficient. Crimes of this kind are referred to as absolute or strict liability offences.

Is there a difference between law and morality?

It is sometimes difficult to draw a clear line between what is criminal and what is immoral. Some actions are obviously both —murder, for example. Others are clearly immoral but not illegal—for example adultery. But there is a grey area in between. Some actions are illegal, because on the whole society disapproves of them on moral or religious grounds, even though they harm no one's life or property. For example a majority of citizens agree that young children should not be exposed to scenes in films depicting extreme violence or overt sexuality, so there are laws and regulations governing this. Other laws involving morality are less easy to justify: blasphemy is still a crime in England, although many people consider that the law should be repealed, especially since it only refers to the Christian religion.

However harmless a thing is, if the law forbids it most people will think it wrong.

W. Somerset Maugham, *British author*

Tort

The commonest types of tort are:

- negligence
- occupier's liability
- trespass
- nuisance
- defamation.

When a crime is committed the state has to ensure that the offender is caught, tried, and, if found guilty, punished. But there are many occasions when the actions of one person, while not necessarily criminal, still injure the health, possessions, or interests of another. For example, while carrying a ladder along the street I may accidentally strike a passer-by and knock them unconscious. As a result they may be unable to work for several weeks. I haven't committed a crime, but my lack of care has caused both physical and financial injury to another. The injured person may then be able to take action in a civil court to claim compensation from the guilty person under the law of tort.

The legal term *tort* comes from a medieval French word meaning 'wrong' or 'injustice'. It is a principle of the legal system that people have a right to security of their persons and property. If that right is infringed, then they are entitled to compensation. (Indeed, if they believe that their rights are about to be infringed they have the right to try to stop it happening.) It follows from this, if my actions injure another person or their property then they have the right to claim compensation from me. It is helpful if such liability can be proved, but sometimes this is not possible—no one can be shown to be liable. In this case, the injured party may be unable to claim any compensation—because there is no one to claim it from.

Strict liability

Sometimes the law says that people are liable when common sense suggests that they are not. Suppose, for example, I own a fierce dog but have put a stout fence round my land and make sure that whenever I go out the gate is securely fastened. I have taken all reasonable precautions. But then the postman comes to the house and leaves the gate open. The dog escapes and attacks an elderly woman in the street. Who is liable? English law holds that this is a case of strict liability and even though I did all I could to stop the event occurring, I am still liable, simply because I owned a dog that was likely to attack people.

Whose fault was that?

Negligence

If someone considers that they have suffered injury, or their property has been damaged, by my actions they can sue me for negligence and claim damages. The person suing becomes the 'claimant' and I become the 'defendant'. This is how it works:

1. The claimant will have to prove that I had a *duty of care*. In other words this was a situation in which I should have taken care not to cause them any harm.

2. They must prove that I was indeed negligent (care*less*).

3. The claimant has to show that the harm caused was a direct result of this lack of care.

4. Finally they must demonstrate that they have suffered some kind of material loss as a result of this. (For example, in the case of a physical injury they might not have been able to work for a period of time.)

In my defence I might be able to argue that no reasonable precautions I could have taken would have stopped the accident occurring; or that the claimant was at the time in the course of committing a crime; or that the claimant was partly or wholly responsible for what happened.

Occupier's liability

If you own land, then you have a liability towards people who enter it to ensure that they don't suffer any harm. So if your roof is in need of repair and a visitor is injured by a falling tile, they may sue you for damages. Even trespassers are covered by this, although the occupier's liability towards them is, not unreasonably, less than it is towards visitors who have a legal right to enter the property.

There is more about trespass in chapter 5. The three different forms of trespass are also defined in the Glossary.

Trespass

The word 'trespass' comes from an Old French word meaning *passing across, passage*. A useful substitute word for its legal meaning might be 'interference'. In English law it comes in three forms: trespass to land (the best known), trespass to goods (interfering with someone else's possessions), trespass to person (which usually takes the form of preventing someone from enjoying freedom of movement—for example by imprisoning them).

There is more about nuisance in chapter 5.

Nuisance

The word 'nuisance' comes from the French word 'nuire', meaning to harm or hurt. This covers any action (often a series of actions) which interfere with someone else's life. For example if a householder operates loud machinery late at night they may well be committing a nuisance because it stops neighbours from sleeping.

There is more about defamation in chapter 9.

Defamation

If you make public a statement that damages someone's reputation, that person may sue you for defamation. You have harmed them personally and they may demand recompense in the form of damages; they will also want the truth made public and some form of apology.

Contract

Adult men and women all over England sign contracts which they do not read, at the behest of canvassers whom they do not know, binding them to pay for articles which they do not want, with money which they have not got.

Sir Gerald Hurst, *British judge*

In our private lives when people make promises we expect them to keep them. Sometimes we are disappointed and we know that some of our acquaintances are more dependable than others. But it wouldn't be possible to run our public lives on this basis. Imagine what would happen if when pay day came round and the boss said, 'I'm sorry I can't pay you this week—I've spent all the payroll money on a new house.'

Public life depends on people making agreements and keeping to them. The two parties involved bind themselves to do something in the future and then expect that this agreement will be fulfilled. Economic and social life would be impossible if we could not trust such a system. Because of this the state provides a guarantee: if one of the parties fails to perform what has been promised, then the other can take action in the courts.

If an agreement is to be legally enforceable, it has to be serious, clearly defined, and intended to be a legal agreement. In addition it has to be of benefit to both parties; there has to be an element of a bargain about it. In English law it does not, on the other hand, need to be written down. You can commit to a contract, as such agreements are known by lawyers, in speech, in writing, or by actions.

The underlying principles of the law are that legally binding agreements should be carried out and if they are not, then the innocent party should not be put at any kind of disadvantage. This can be achieved in a number of ways: for example, by forcing the other party to perform their side of the bargain; by requiring them to provide a substitute; or by requiring monetary compensation.

Words are a lawyer's tools of trade.

Lord Denning, *British judge and Master of the Rolls*

What the law means by a contract

In a true contract:

- there have to be two parties to the agreement;
- the agreement must be meant to be legally binding;
- there has to be some kind of exchange of goods or services.

The law says that there have to be to be the following five essential components:

1 **Offer**
One party says in effect, 'If you accept this offer, I will do X.' This must be seriously intended and can be in speech, writing, or through some kind of action. (For example if, in London, a large red bus with a sign saying 'Marble Arch' stops at the bus stop for me to get on, that can be regarded as a seriously intended offer to take me to Marble Arch if I pay the fare.)

2 **Acceptance**
The other party has to accept the whole of the offer. If they say they accept a modified version of it, that isn't an acceptance, but a counter-offer. Once they have accepted, a contract exists between the two parties. The acceptance is normally in the same form as the offer: speech, writing, or action. (So, to continue the example, if I get on the bus it is an acceptance of the offer and an understanding that I will fulfil my part of the bargain—to pay the fare required to get to Marble Arch.)

Acceptance
The publishers of computer software sometimes make use of the performance of an action as an acceptance of a contract. The disk containing the software is sealed in an envelope or case. When you break the seal you are acknowledging that you accept the terms and conditions of the software user agreement.

3 **Consideration**
The agreement has to involve an *exchange of consideration*. This means that money, goods, or services —or some combination of the three—has to pass from A to B and from B to A. So, in the example the consideration offered by the bus company is to carry me to Marble Arch; in return I offer the consideration of the fare. Money has been exchanged for services.

4 **Intention**
The parties must have the intention to enter into a contract that is legally binding. If the contract concerns a business relationship, the law assumes that this is the intention unless the parties state otherwise.

5 **Capacity**
Each of the two parties has to be able to understand what they are undertaking. If you are over eighteen it is assumed you can do this unless it can be proved that at the time of engaging in the contract you were mentally incapable or drunk *and* that the other party knew this *and* that the goods or services you were being offered were 'luxuries' rather than 'necessaries'. 'Necessaries' are things required by the person involved for the maintenance of their ordinary life. The law takes the view that these differ from person to person. So, for example, an elaborate walking stick with a silver handle might be a 'necessary' for a wealthy elderly person, while it would be a luxury for a healthy and impoverished teenager. If the goods or services offered were necessaries then you will have to pay for them.

Capacity
. . . the ability or power to do, experience, or understand something . . . a person's legal competence . . .

New Oxford Dictionary of English.

The terms of the contract

Central to a contract are the promises, descriptions, and conditions agreed by the parties. These are called the *terms* of the contract. They are of two kinds:

- **Express terms**
  These are the terms that the parties have discussed and expressed in speech or writing. They are particular to the specific contract.

- **Implied terms**
  These are terms which are not in the contract itself but which are implied by the law of the land (e.g. laws about employment conditions) or by tradition or custom (e.g. what has always been done in a traditional local market). It is also possible for a court to interpret what the parties must have intended by their contract, even if the words didn't actually say that.

The minute you read something you can't understand, you can almost be sure it was drawn up by a lawyer.

Will Rogers, *American entertainer*

Discharge of a contract

A contract can be ended or 'discharged' in one of four ways:

- **Performance**
  As the name suggests, this means that the two parties both do exactly what they said they would do.

- **Agreement**
  The parties agree not to perform exactly what they said they would do. (For example they perform most of what the contract sets out and agree to forget about the rest of it.)

- **Frustration**
  It becomes impossible (for example through a change in the law or the death of one of the parties) to perform.

- **Breach of Contract**
  One of the parties fails to perform and the other sues for breach of contract. If breach of contract is proved, the defendant then has to pay damages to the complainant. These are limited to the amount of actual financial loss. Sometimes a contract will specify the amount of damages, in order to avoid lengthy and expensive litigation. These 'liquidated damages' should reflect the likely amount of financial loss. If they are much higher and are put into the contract to punish the defaulter, this is known as a penalty clause. Courts will not enforce penalty clauses, limiting damages to the amount actually lost.

The legal system

3

CONTENTS

Where the laws come from

In England there are three main types of law: statute law, common law, and European Union law.

Statute law

In theory the Legislature (Parliament) makes laws which are administered by the Executive (Her Majesty's Government) and when there are disputes they are decided upon by the Judiciary (the judges and the courts). In fact most legislation originates with the Government, which also oversees and pays for the administration of justice. Nevertheless it is an important principle of English law that the Judiciary is completely independent of the Executive.

Most new laws are initiated by the Government, although a few come from individual Members of Parliament (Private Members' Bills). A bill is drafted and placed before Parliament. It receives three 'readings' in the House of Commons, during which it is scrutinized in detail and amended, before passing on to the House of Lords which examines it in similar detail and may reject it all or in part. If this happens it returns to the Commons, which may accept the Lords' decision, or may insist that they reconsider. Ultimately the Lords cannot prevent the Commons from passing a bill, but they can delay the process —even to the extent that the bill is lost through lack of time. Once a bill has passed through all its stages in Parliament it goes to the Queen for the Royal Assent, at which point it becomes an Act of Parliament and the law of the land.

Common law

Not all precedents are good precedents, and the fact that it has been done before indicates that it is high time we stopped doing it now.

Lord Simon

As we saw on the previous page, to all intents and purposes the word 'statute' means the same as 'Act of Parliament'.

Much of the English Constitution is unwritten, having developed in response to events over the centuries. Something similar is true of the common law. As situations have arisen in which people have been in dispute, judges have been asked to adjudicate. If no law exists covering the exact details of the case, they make a judgment based on cases that are comparable. These written judgments have accumulated to form the common law. Where a litigant is unhappy with the judge's ruling, he or she may appeal to a higher court. If this makes a different judgment, then that in turn becomes part of the law. A lower court cannot overturn the judgment of a higher, so that the judgments of the highest court in the land, the House of Lords, are always supreme. The only way in which its judgments can be overturned is by the passing of a new statute by Parliament.

The beauty of the common law: it is a maze, not a motorway.

Lord Diplock

European Union Law

In 1972 the United Kingdom entered the European Community (now the European Union). When Parliament passed legislation to this effect, it diminished its own powers, because European Community law is superior to national law.

European Institutions

There are four E.U. institutions involved in European law.

The Commission

The European Commission is the E.U.'s civil service. It is headed by twenty Commissioners appointed by the member states. Each Commissioner takes responsibility for a particular department (Directorate General) with responsibilities covering a defined sector of the E.U.'s activities.

The Commission's role is to prepare and recommend legislation for debate and decision by the Council of Ministers. Sometimes this process is initiated by the Council, but is frequently begun by the Commission itself. In a small number of well-defined areas the Commission can legislate on its own authority. The Commission also has responsibility for checking that member states obey E.U. laws and, if necessary, it refers law-breaking states to the European Court of Justice.

The European Parliament

Members of the Parliament are directly elected by the citizens of the E.U. The Parliament is consulted about proposed legislation by the Council of Ministers, but, while it can express its opinion, it has very limited powers to change legislation. It does, however, have the power to accept or reject the annual budget.

E.U. milestones

1957
Treaty of Rome: European Economic Community founded

1967
Formation of the European Community (France, W. Germany, Belgium, Luxembourg, Italy, Netherlands)

1973
UK, Ireland, Denmark join

1981
Greece joins

1986
Spain and Portugal join

1991
Maastricht Treaty

1995
Austria, Finland, Sweden join

1999
Introduction of the Euro

The Council of Ministers

The real power lies with the Council of Ministers (formally the Council of the European Union), which debates and passes legislation. Each member state appoints a minister to represent it at its meetings (normally, but not always, the foreign minister). States have a number of votes proportionate to their size.

The European Court of Justice

If states break E.U. law they can be referred to the European Court of Justice. The Court makes judgments in disputes between European institutions, between these institutions and member states, and between member states. It also provides guidance to the courts of individual states on matters of European law. It should not be confused with the European Court of Human Rights.

There is more about the **European Court of Human Rights** in chapter 9 on page 88.

European Law

European Union law is superior to the law of individual member states; in other words, if there is a conflict between the law of a state and that of the E.U., then the E.U. has to be obeyed. European law can take four forms.

Treaties

(Such as the Maastricht Treaty.) These are major agreements between the nations comprising the E.U., which have to be ratified (approved) nationally and then passed into national law.

Regulations

These have the effect of law in member states (although they may require legislation in some states—for example when they contradict existing national legislation).

Directives

These require individual member states to interpret and enforce their provisions (which will usually mean passing national laws).

Decisions of the European Court of Justice

As we have seen, the Court has the role of interpreting E.U. law and its decisions are then binding on member states.

In Germany, under the law everything is prohibited except that which is permitted. In France, everything is permitted except that which is prohibited. In the Soviet Union, everything is prohibited, including that which is permitted. And in Italy, everything is permitted, especially that which is prohibited.

Newton Minow

The Criminal Courts

I think crime pays. The hours are good. You travel a lot.

Woody Allen, *American film actor and director*

Criminal cases can be heard in two types of court:

Magistrates' Courts

These are local courts where cases are heard by a panel of magistrates, or Justices of the Peace. They are lay people (i.e. they do not have any legal qualifications) who give their time voluntarily to determine certain types of case. The prosecution, represented by a solicitor or barrister from the Crown Prosecution Service, outlines the case and then calls witnesses to prove it. Witnesses can be cross-examined by the defence. The defence then presents its case in a similar way, after which the magistrates confer and give their verdict. Between a guilty verdict and the sentence the defence can enter a plea 'in mitigation'—a reasoned request that the sentence should not be too harsh because of the defendant's previous good record and/or present circumstances. The magistrates may then call for medical or social reports before passing sentence. They then either pass sentence themselves, or, if they think it merits a more severe sentence than they can deliver, pass the case on to the Crown Court for sentencing.

Crown Courts

A jury consists of twelve persons chosen to decide who has the better lawyer.

Robert Frost, *American poet*

In a Crown Court cases are heard by a judge and a jury of twelve adults whose names are taken from the electoral register. As in a Magistrates' Court the prosecution case is followed by the defence case. In each witnesses may be called, examined, cross-examined, and re-examined. After the two sides have been presented, each advocate has a chance to speak to the jury, reiterating the main features of the case. The judge then sums up the facts of the case and explains the relevant law to the jurors. The jury then retires to consider its verdict. This should be unanimous but, if that proves impossible, the judge may allow a majority verdict, with which at least ten of the twelve must agree. If even that proves impossible, then the jury are dismissed and a fresh trial becomes necessary.

What is tried where?

Criminal offences are divided into three categories:

- **Summary**
  At the lowest level are the 'small' or summary offences, which receive the summary justice of the Magistrates' Court. These include such things as common assault and careless driving.

- **Indictable**
  At the other end of the scale come much more serious offences such as robbery with violence, rape, and murder. These have to be tried in a Crown Court in front of a jury.

- **Triable either way**
  In between come a range of offences which can be tried either in a Magistrates' Court, or a Crown Court. These include dangerous driving and theft. The defence and the prosecution both have the right to say in which type of court they think the case should be tried. In the past this has often meant that defendants, especially those charged with motoring offences, have opted for trial by jury in a Crown Court, in the belief that this offers a better chance of acquittal. This right is under attack and may, in the future, be curtailed.

Examples

Summary

- Common assault
- Drink driving
- Driving without insurance
- Criminal damage up to £5,000

Indictable

- Robbery
- Rape
- Murder

Triable either way

- Theft
- Assault causing actual bodily harm

kleptomaniac: *a person who helps himself because he cannot help himself.*

Anonymous

Appeals

If the accused is found guilty, then he or she may have the right to appeal to the next court up in the chain:

Supreme Court?

As this book was going to press, the Government announced that it intended to replace the House of Lords with a Supreme Court as the final court of appeal.

Civil cases

Civil cases can be brought by individuals, companies, and organizations. The individual bringing the action is referred to as the *claimant* (previously the 'plaintiff') and the individual defending it as the *defendant*. The majority of civil cases in which one individual sues another fall into two categories:

- **Breach of contract**
  If I arrange with you to paint your house and you agree to pay me £2,000 for the work, we have made a contract (even if it is not written down). If I do the work and you fail to pay me, then you have broken the contract and I am entitled to go to court to recover the money you owe me.

There is more about tort in chapter 2 on pages 14-16.

- **Tort**
  'Tort' comes from the French word for 'wrong' and that is its meaning in the law. There are a number of torts for which an individual can sue another. These include assault, negligence, and defamation.

Court cases are expensive, so claimants and defendants will often seek to resolve their disputes without actually going to court. This is particularly true in breach of contract cases. If this proves impossible, then the case goes to court, but to which court it goes depends on the nature of the action.

Magistrates' Court

Certain civil cases are heard in Magistrates' Courts. These include failure to pay income tax, VAT, or council tax; the licensing of clubs and pubs; and a variety of family cases including maintenance payments, and the welfare of children.

County Court

A large number of cases are conducted in the County Court, including personal injuries, debt, racial and sexual discrimination, and undefended divorce cases.

High Court

More serious civil cases go to the High Court. This has three Divisions:

- **Family Division**
  As its name suggests, this court handles cases involving personal relationships within the family: divorces that are too complex for the County Court, adoption, and wardship. (When there is a dispute over who should legally have responsibility for a child, and in some other situations, a child may be made a *ward of court*. The court then has legal responsibility and can determine who should care for the child.)

- **Queen's Bench Division**
  The most high profile cases heard in this court are those concerned with defamation. It also handles serious compensation claims and judicial reviews.

- **Chancery Division**
  The Chancery Division deals with contested wills, bankruptcies, and cases in which tax payers have a major disagreement with the Inland Revenue over tax liability.

Civil cases are normally heard by a judge without a jury. The judge is responsible for the whole conduct of the case, much of which takes place before the formal hearing. Cases are conducted under the Civil Procedure Rules, which aim to produce a fair, efficient, and economic administration of justice. This often means avoiding a formal hearing altogether. Depending on the size of the claim, a case can follow one of three *tracks*. These are, in increasing size and complexity: small claims, fast track, and multi-track.

Different tracks

small claims
amounts up to £5,000

fast track
amounts between £5,000 and £15,000

multi-track
amounts over £15,000

See note on page 27

As with criminal cases, there is a system of appeals: from the County Court to the High Court or the Court of Appeal; from the High Court to the Court of Appeal, and thence to the House of Lords.

The lawyers

A lawyer is someone who makes sure he gets what's coming to you.

Anonymous (USA)

The hierarchy of courts and tribunals which administer the law provide a living for a multitude of legal professionals. Some, like judges and clerks, are directly involved in the machine itself. Many others, like solicitors and barristers, advise and represent individuals, groups, and organizations in their encounters with the law.

In English law there is a traditional distinction between the two main types of lawyer you could consult: in the past if you wanted someone to speak on your behalf in court you went to a barrister; otherwise you went to a solicitor. Today things are more complex. Solicitors have the right to plead a case in certain courts, and trained paralegals conduct a lot of the business formerly done by solicitors.

Barristers

bar
An imaginary barrier in a court of law. Only Queen's Counsel, officers of the court, and litigants in person are allowed between the bar and the bench when the court is in session.

bench
Literally the seat of a judge in court.

As the name suggests, a *bar*rister is someone who pleads at the *bar*, the place where cases are heard. Barristers belong to one of the four Inns of Court. Before being *called to the bar* they will have spent three years at university studying for a law degree (or a university degree in another subject followed by a year's 'conversion course'). Then they spend some time as the pupil of an established barrister, before gaining a position as a junior barrister. After increasing in experience and reputation they may be selected as a *Queen's Counsel* (QC). QCs are barristers with at least ten years' experience and are chosen by the Lord Chancellor.

QC?
The office of Queen's Counsel is currently being reviewed and could even be abolished, like that of the Lord Chancellor (see note on page 32).

Barristers belong to a *chambers* which is where they have their offices and by which they are given their *briefs*, instructions from solicitors to conduct a case on behalf of a client. They have the right to appear as an advocate in any court or tribunal. Barristers can also be asked to give a legal opinion, an authoritative statement of the law in a particular situation. This is based on their knowledge of the law, and their experience as advocates. It tells the client what they believe would be the result, should a case come to trial.

Solicitors

Individuals and organizations who need legal advice normally go first to a solicitor. Like barristers, solicitors spend three years at university leading to a law degree (or a university degree in another subject followed by a year's 'conversion course'). They then do a year's legal practice course, leading to an examination. After that they spend a further period employed under a training contract before becoming fully qualified solicitors.

In England and Wales there are approximately 85,000 practising solicitors (compared to about 9,000 barristers). In the past they could not act as advocates, but now they can do so, working independently or with a barrister. They may still not, however, appear in the higher courts.

Many solicitors used to regard themselves as generalists, providing advice and services over the whole range of legal problems faced by clients. Increasingly today they specialize in one or more aspects of the law. This is particularly the case in large companies and partnerships, where clients will be directed to the solicitor specializing in the field that is relevant to their needs.

Paralegals

Increasingly firms of solicitors are using the services of paralegals, who have a legal training (commonly a law degree), but have not yet qualified as solicitors. Legal work is increasingly complex and specialized, so paralegals will focus on their own area of expertise, for example conveyancing (the legal side of selling property) or personal injury compensation claims. Some will later go on to qualify as solicitors, while others will prefer to remain as paralegals.

Magistrates and judges

Lord Chancellor?
As this book was going to press, the Government announced that it was abolishing the post of Lord Chancellor. The job of appointing judges would be given to a newly created Commission.

Magistrates

Magistrates are also known as Justices of the Peace (or JPs). There are over 30,000 magistrates in England and between them they try 95% of criminal cases. It is true to say that without this body of volunteers, the legal system would grind to a halt. Almost all magistrates are unpaid volunteers, but there are a small number of paid (*stipendiary*) magistrates, working in large centres of population. They are in effect junior judges and are officially called *district judges (Magistrates' Court)*.

The unpaid magistrates are a group of men and women who have no formal legal qualifications. They are selected by the Lord Chancellor through local advisory panels—at the rate of about 1,600 a year. They receive a certain amount of basic training, and are assisted in their work by legally qualified *justices' clerks*, solicitors or barristers who ensure that the work of the Magistrates' Courts runs smoothly and that the magistrates receive the guidance and support they need. The clerks' guidance is restricted to advice about the law; they may not comment on the facts of a particular case being tried.

Judges

Four things belong to a judge: to hear courteously, to answer wisely, to consider soberly, and to decide impartially.

Socrates, *Greek philosopher*

As we have seen, there is a hierarchy of courts, going up from the lowest, the Magistrates' Court, to the highest, the House of Lords, the final court of appeal. The ranks of judges mirror this hierarchy. At the lowest level are part-timers, the *recorders*, and at the top we have the *Law Lords*. The table opposite shows the different types of judge and the kinds of case with which they can be concerned.

Judges are drawn from the ranks of barristers and solicitors, mostly barristers. Some begin by getting a taste of the job by working as recorders, part-time judges trying cases for twenty or more days a year. Judges are appointed by the Lord Chancellor and receive a brief period of training involving both tuition and sentencing exercises in which new judges consider hypothetical but realistic cases and discuss what sentence the defendant should receive.

High Court judges may have come up through the ranks, but many are appointed direct from the pool of distinguished and experienced Queen's Counsels. Very few solicitors are appointed as High Court judges, although it can happen.

Name	Court	Number*	Types of case
Magistrate	Magistrates' Court	30,000	Minor criminal & civil
Recorder	County/ Crown	1,350	(part-time) criminal/civil
District judge	County	400	civil (especially small claims)
Circuit judge	County/ Crown	560	serious criminal lesser civil
High Court judge	High	100	more serious civil cases
Appeal Court judge	Appeal	35	Appeals from County, Crown, & High Courts
Law Lord	House of Lords†	12	Appeals from Appeal Court

* These are only approximate and can vary. They refer to England and Wales.

How do you address a judge?

District judge: Sir/Madam

Circuit judge: Your Honour

High Court judge and above: My Lord / My Lady

†See note on page 27

Yes, I could have been a judge but I never had the Latin, never had the Latin for the judging, I just never had sufficient of it to get through the rigorous judging exams. They're noted for their rigour. People come out staggering and saying, 'My God, what a rigorous exam'—and so I became a miner instead . . . I'd rather have been a judge than a miner. Being a miner, as soon as you are too old and tired and sick and stupid to do the job properly, you have to go. Well, the opposite applies with judges.

Peter Cook, *British humorist*

The Crown Prosecution Service

The other major 'player' in the criminal justice system is the Crown Prosecution Service, often simply referred to as the CPS. It is responsible for organizing most criminal prosecutions, under the Director of Public Prosecutions. The CPS is independent of the police, with whom, of course, it has to work closely.

Outside the court system

Not all occasions on which a wrong has been committed end up in the court system. There are two important ways in which it is possible to seek justice outside the courts.

Tribunals

Tribunal
The word 'tribunal' has its origins in the history of the Roman Empire, where a tribunal was 'a raised semicircular or square platform in a Roman basilica, on which the seats of the magistrates were placed' (*Oxford English Dictionary*). From this it came to mean a 'judgement seat' and then the place you went to get a judgement.

In a number of important areas the government has set up administrative tribunals to make judgments in cases referred to them by individuals or organizations. The tribunal system covers a wide range of subjects, including:

- Pensions
- Employment
- Social Security
- Income Tax

Different tribunals work in different ways, but an employment tribunal is typical of many. Employees who feel that they have been unfairly dismissed, or treated wrongly in such matters as redundancy, equal pay, or maternity benefits can take their case to a tribunal. At the tribunal they put their case to a panel composed of a legally qualified Chairman and two independent laypeople. They can speak for themselves or can have legal representation. The case for the employer is put in a similar way and both sides can be questioned by the members of the tribunal. Although this parallels the adversarial pattern of a trial in court, there is much less formality. Once both sides have been heard, the tribunal can award compensation or some other judgment. (So if an employee has been unfairly dismissed, they can insist that they are reinstated.) The only appeal that is possible against a tribunal decision is on a matter of law, so you cannot appeal if you think the award is too harsh, for example.

Ombudsmen

It is also possible, in certain areas of life, to make a formal complaint to an ombudsman. If, for example, you feel that you have been treated with rudeness and/or inefficiency by employees at your local council, you may be entitled to make a formal complaint to the Local Government Ombudsman (or Commissioner, as the post is more formally known).

The list of ombudsmen is large and growing. It includes:

- **The Parliamentary Ombudsman**
  (The Parliamentary Commissioner for Administration, who deals with complaints against government departments.)
- **The Health Service Ombudsman**
- **The Broadcasting Standards Commission**
- **The Police Complaints Authority**

When someone approaches an ombudsman it is normally after they have exhausted all other possibilities. For example, if you wish to complain about the way your local doctor or nurse has treated you, you must first seek satisfaction from the local medical practice, and if that doesn't work, you should request an independent review panel. If that request is refused you have to go to the local Community Health Council. It is only after that stage that you can go to the ombudsman. In addition, you can only use this approach if there is no other remedy under the law. If, for example, it would be possible to sue for negligence, then you cannot go to the ombudsman.

Origins
The idea of an ombudsman, an official charged with the role of overseeing the administration of justice comes from Sweden. It was copied by Finland in 1919, Denmark in 1954, and by Norway and New Zealand in 1962. Since then the idea has been adopted in many different countries around the world.

Britain's first ombudsman was appointed in 1967.

4 From cradle to grave

CONTENTS

Living together

We saw in Chapter 1 that one purpose of the law is to provide us with a framework within which we can make our own private arrangements. Although we may regard our private lives as entirely our own affair, in fact they affect a range of people close to us and not so close. Since things can go wrong, there are many occasions when the law can be involved. Where emotions are concerned, it is when things go wrong that we are often at our most vulnerable and least rational. So, for example, when a marriage breaks down, the law provides a framework within which practical arrangements can be made.

The law is also a means of compulsion. This is particularly important when it comes to protecting the weak. A marriage may be regarded as a private arrangement between two adults, and its possible breakdown is something for which they have to be prepared and which they must negotiate themselves. Children, on the other hand, have no choice in the matter; they cannot look after themselves and need the law to protect their interests.

The ways in which people choose to arrange their personal lives do not, however, stand still. A hundred years ago marriage was the norm and couples who chose to live together and remain unmarried were rare. Now, increasingly the opposite is true; 40% of all children are now born outside marriage. In a time of rapidly changing social customs, the law has to catch up as best it can. The result is that new laws are enacted quite frequently, but never quickly enough to deal with the real world of living relationships.

Marriage

In England couples can be married by a Registrar, an Anglican priest, or by any other person who has a certificate to do so. The ceremony can take place in a registry office, Anglican church, or other approved place. Since the Marriage Act of 1994 it is possible to be married in a variety of places: golf clubs, castles, football clubs, even Alexandra Palace and the London Zoo have been approved for this purpose. The couple to be married must be unmarried, over eighteen (or over sixteen, with their parents' consent), of the opposite sex, and entering into the marriage of their own free will. Also they must not be closely related.

Bigamy is having one wife too many. Monogamy is the same.

Anonymous

When people are married they acquire new rights and duties. Specifically they undertake to live together, to support each other financially, and, by implication, to have sexual relations with each other. This duty of cohabitation (sometimes referred to in the law by the Latin term *consortium*) is not precisely defined in the law, for the very good reason that human relationships as intimate as marriage defy precise and detailed definitions. On the other hand, when a marriage breaks down it is because cohabitation is no longer possible for some reason.

Cohabitation

In legal terms there is no such thing as a 'common law marriage', although the phrase is still used to describe the *cohabitation* of a man and woman who are not married (*cohabitants* in legal terms). There are similarities and differences between the rights and responsibilities of married couples and cohabitants. Some of these are set out in the table on the next two pages.

Gay and Lesbian couples
The rights of same-sex couples are the subject of changes in the law proposed by the Government in June 2003.

Useful web sites

The Citizens' Advice Bureaux web site (http://www.adviceguide.org.uk) contains useful guidance on the legal similarities and differences between marriage and cohabitation. For this and other similar resources, see page 153.

	Married couples
Legal status	The status of a couple who are legally married is recognized by the law.
Housing	Both partners have the right to live in the marital home.
Children	Both parents have parental responsibility—even after divorce. Both parents are responsible for financial support of children. Husband assumed to be the father of children born during the marriage unless it is proved otherwise.
Adoption	May adopt as a couple.
Wills	If either partner dies without making a will the other will inherit part or all of their estate.
Support	Each is obliged to support the other financially.
Banking and money	If the couple have a joint account each has full rights to the money in it. On the death of one, the other has full access to the account. If each has a single account, on the death of one the bank may allow the other access to the balance if it is small; otherwise it is part of the estate and subject to probate.
Pension schemes	Occupational and personal pension schemes have to provide for the married partner of the person whose pension it is; if that person dies, then the partner is provided for. Provision is also usually made for children.

Unmarried couples

Unmarried couples who are cohabiting (living together as a couple) do not have one defined legal status. The law treats them differently in different circumstances. Some couples choose to draw up and sign a cohabitation agreement, although it is not clear whether such agreements can be enforced. Some, but not all, of the definitions that follow apply to gay and lesbian couples.	**Legal status**
If one partner is sole tenant or owner of the home, then the other partner has no right to stay in it.	**Housing**
Mother has sole responsibility unless she makes a formal agreement with the father, or exceptionally, a court makes the father responsible. Both parents are responsible for financial support of children. Male partner is not assumed to be the father of any children born during the relationship.	**Children**
May not adopt as a couple. One partner acting alone may adopt.	**Adoption**
If either partner dies without making a will the other partner will not automatically inherit anything.	**Wills**
Neither is obliged to support the other.	**Support**
If the couple have a joint account, each has full rights to the money in it. On the death of one, the other has full access to the account. If each has a single account, then on the death of one, the other has no access.	**Banking and money**
It depends on the particular scheme. Some make provision for unmarried heterosexual partners and a few for gay and lesbian partners.	**Pension schemes**

Children

The law relating to children is in a state of rapid change. This is partly because children are now brought up in many different family environments; single-parent families are commonplace. So the law has to adapt to these altered circumstances. There is also a growing concern with the ways in which children are being drawn into anti-social and criminal behaviour.

At the centre of the law relating to children is the concept of responsibility. Whatever the family circumstances into which a child is born, someone assumes a range of duties and powers referred to by the law as *parental responsibility*. This involves such obvious and necessary things as:

- **registering the child's birth**
  This must be done within six weeks of the birth, by going to the District Registrar for Births, Marriages, and Deaths. The birth can be registered by the mother or by the father, if he is married to the mother. The information recorded includes the place and date of birth, the mother's details (and, if the parents are married, the father's) and the child's sex and given names.

- **making sure that the child is properly fed, clothed, and looked after**

- **taking care of the child's health**
  This includes the right to consent to or refuse medical treatment. When parents have religious or other beliefs which entail the refusal of medical treatment, this can lead to conflict, and the medical authorities may inform the Local Authority's Social Services Department that the child's health and safety are at risk. If the Authority agrees with this assessment, this may lead to a court order giving permission for the medical treatment to be carried out against the parents' wishes.

- **ensuring that the child is educated**
  The law requires that children between the ages of five and sixteen receive full-time education at a state school or in

some other way: at a fee-paying school, by a private tutor, or by the parents themselves. Local Authorities have a responsibility to ensure that children in their area are properly educated and have the right to inspect any private arrangement parents may make. If a child is educated at a state school then he or she will have to follow the National Curriculum; otherwise not.

For every person who wants to teach there are approximately thirty who don't want to learn—much.

W. C. Sellar and R. J. Yeatman, *British authors*

If the child's parents are married, then both parents have parental responsibility and retain it, even if they later divorce. If the parents are unmarried, then the mother alone has parental responsibility and the father only has it if he and the mother sign an agreement to this effect, or if a court orders it. The unmarried father does, however, have the legal duty to maintain the child and may be chased up (with varying degrees of success) by the Child Support Agency if he fails to do so. The Child Support, Pensions, and Social Security Act 2002 sets out how much an unmarried father should pay to support his child(ren). If he has three or more children, then he may have to pay the maximum amount of 25% of his net income (after tax and National Insurance).

The Local Authority

The Local Authority has a responsibility for all children who live within its area. This is exercised normally through its Social Services Department. If they suspect that a child is suffering, or is likely to suffer, significant harm, then they have a legal duty to investigate the case. After investigating they may decide to apply to the court (normally the Family Proceedings Court) for the child to be taken into care. This is a fairly longwinded process and for more urgent cases (where, for example, social workers are being prevented from even seeing a child) the court may issue an *Emergency Protection Order* which allows for the child to be removed from the control of the parents while the situation is assessed.

Go directly—see what she's doing, and tell her she mustn't.

Punch (1872)

When children are allowed to do what

So far we have just referred to 'children', but the ages at which young children are restricted from doing things adults can do vary considerably. The list that follows is only a small selection:

At 10 a child can:
- be convicted of a crime (but see below)
- open a bank account

At 14 a child can:
- own an airgun
- go into a bar with an adult (but not drink alcohol)
- take on a part-time job

At 16 a child can:
- buy cigarettes, fireworks, or premium bonds
- marry (with parental consent)
- join the armed forces (with parental consent)
- drive a tractor or fly a glider solo

At 17 a child can:
- drive a car
- give blood

At 18 a child can do anything an adult can, except:
- stand as a candidate in local or national elections
- drive a bus (or heavy goods vehicle)
- apply for a licence to sell alcohol.

Crime

Children under ten years of age cannot be tried for a crime. The only remedy for children so young who persistently break the law is for them to be taken into care. After the age of ten children can be charged with a crime and may be found guilty if the court considers that the child was aware that the action for which they are being tried was seriously wrong. From the age of fourteen children are considered to be morally responsible.

There is this horrible idea, beginning with Jean-Jacques Rousseau and still going strong in college classrooms that natural man is naturally good . . . Anybody who's ever met a toddler knows this is nonsense.

P. J. O'Rourke

Up to the age of seventeen, young persons who are suspected of a crime, or who may have witnessed one are treated somewhat differently from adults. If they are taken to a police station to be questioned, this must be done in the presence of an *appropriate adult*. This will often be a parent, but if the parent is unavailable or unsuitable (for example because of mental incapacity) then it may be someone from the Local Authority Social Services Department. Indeed any adult unconnected with the police may be an appropriate adult, depending on circumstances.

If a young person admits to committing a crime then unless it is a serious offence such as rape or arson the police have some freedom of action. Rather than prosecuting, they may decide to give the young offender a caution—effectively a serious telling-off—which does not go down on the individual's record, but can be mentioned in any future hearing in a Youth Court.

If the young person does not admit the offence, then the police must decide whether to prosecute. If they do, then the case will usually be heard before specially trained magistrates in a Youth Court. Sentences available to the magistrates range from a custodial sentence in a young offenders' institution to a supervision order, which is the equivalent to probation for ten- to sixteen-year-olds.

Divorce

He taught me housekeeping; when I divorce, I keep the house.

American film star Zsa Zsa Gabor *of her fifth husband*

When a marriage does break down, it often, but not always, leads to divorce. A couple may decide to live apart, which can be arranged informally by mutual agreement, or more formally by means of a legal document that both parties sign. This can be a useful way of dealing with the practical aspects of a possibly painful situation. More often than not, however, a broken marriage leads to divorce. Divorce is possible for couples who have been married for at least a year and whose marriage has irretrievably broken down. There are five proofs that this has happened:

1 One of the partners has committed adultery and this is intolerable to the other.

2 One of the partners is guilty of 'unreasonable behaviour' to the extent that the other partner cannot reasonably be expected to continue to live with them.

3 One of the partners deserts the other for a period of two years or more.

4 The two partners are separated for at least two years and both agree to a divorce.

5 The two partners are separated for five years or more (i.e. without the need for mutual consent).

A partner seeking a divorce can do so with or without the aid of a solicitor. Couples are encouraged to consider the possibility of reconciliation using the services of a professional mediator. If this is not possible then the petition for divorce is handled by the Divorce County Court. The exact procedure will depend on whether both partners have agreed that they want a divorce and whether there are children. The case is considered by the district judge, who will, after the necessary formalities have been completed, issue a decree nisi. Six weeks and a day after that the couple can apply for a decree absolute and the marriage is dissolved.

Decree nisi
'Nisi' is the Latin for 'unless'. A decree nisi says that unless any objections are made, the divorce will be completed within a set period.

Divorce practicalities

Before that, of course, a large number of practical matters have to be decided. Custody and maintenance of any children come first (see page 41), but even where there are no children, the court has to decide how the couple's property is to be divided and what maintenance, if any, will be due from one partner to the other. This is not, as is sometimes thought, a straight 50/50 division. In making a judgment, the court will take into account how long the couple have been married, their ages, their ability to earn a living to support themselves, and so on. To take an extreme example, if the couple have only been married for just over a year and the wife was already very wealthy while the husband was penniless at the time of the marriage, it would be unreasonable for him to expect to walk off with half his ex-wife's property. On the other hand the couple did live together as husband and wife, and the court may decide that if the husband is, for example, unable to work the wife should contribute to his maintenance.

Conduct
It is not necessarily the case that the actions of one partner, which may have led to the divorce (such as adultery) are taken into account when the court is deciding issues such as the division of property. It doesn't normally say, for example, 'The wife committed adultery, so she shall receive £25,000 less.' The approach taken is much more to avoid apportioning blame; the conduct of either partner is usually only taken into account in settlements when that conduct has been extreme.

What about the children?

Married parents who wish to divorce are required to try to agree on the arrangements they are going to make for their children. One of the papers they have to submit when applying for a divorce is a *statement of arrangements*. In this they have to set out, among other things:

- where the child will live;
- where he or she will be educated;
- who will look after him or her (and when, if the care is to be shared);
- how the child's upbringing is to be financed;
- arrangements for visiting.

If the parents can agree on all this, then the district judge has only to examine the detailed arrangements to ensure that they are reasonable.

Court orders

If parents who are separating can agree a reasonable plan for the care of their children, then generally the courts will support them. When they cannot do so, then the court will impose a solution that is in the best interest of the children. It has four orders it can impose which will, between them, cover all aspects of the care of the children:

- **Residence order**
  The court can order that the children should live with one or other of the parents, or both on a shared basis, or some other responsible adult such as a grandparent.

- **Contact order**
  This ensures that the parent with whom the child is not living can have access to him or her. The responsibility is on the person the child is living with to arrange this. It can involve visits, periods staying with the other parent, or telephone calls.

- **Prohibited steps order**
  This allows the court to prevent either of the parents from behaving in a particular way without the court's consent. So, for example, it might be decided that one parent should not have access to the child and should be prevented from attempting to visit.

- **Specific issue order**
  This is a catch-all allowing the court to deal with any issue that it needs to. For example, in the case of a dispute between the parents about which school a child should go to, the court can order that he or she should attend a particular school.

What happens when someone dies

When someone dies, their death has to be reported to the Registrar of Births, Marriages, and Deaths. The Registrar will need a certificate stating the time and cause of death. This is issued by either a doctor or coroner. If the person died at home and the doctor had been attending them during an illness which led to their death, then the doctor will issue a sealed death certificate to take to the Registrar. If the doctor's last attendance on the dead person was more than two weeks before the death, or if the death was unexpected, or the result of an accident of violence, then the doctor will report it to the coroner. Much the same applies to deaths in hospital, with the addition that if the patient died during an operation it has to be reported to the coroner.

The coroner will normally order a post mortem examination and if the circumstances warrant it will hold an inquest. Normally there is no jury, and the coroner directs proceedings, taking evidence from witnesses. These can be questioned by anyone who has a *proper interest*—for example, relatives or insurance companies. At the end of the hearing, if the coroner is satisfied he or she will record a verdict and inform the Registrar of the findings.

The office of coroner

The earliest references to coroners date back to the 12th century. The *coronator* or *crowner* was elected by the free landowners of a county to protect crown property. The original idea of the office was to balance the power of the sheriff, who might work against the interests of the crown and in those of powerful local feudal lords. As power moved away from the crown and towards Parliament, many of the coroner's original functions disappeared. By the early years of the 20th century coroners had only the functions they have today. They enquire into violent or unexpected deaths, or deaths in other legally defined circumstances. Coroners have to have a legal or medical qualification. Many are solicitors, but doctors are also appointed coroners.

Inheritance

You know what they say, if at first you don't succeed, you're not the eldest son.

Stephen Fry, *British writer and entertainer*

If someone dies without making a will (or the will cannot be found), they are said to have died *intestate*. In such cases the law states that the dead person's *estate* is distributed between a surviving husband or wife (*spouse*), children and grandchildren (*issue*), and possibly other relatives (but not if there are any surviving issue). The proportions of this distribution are set down by law.

Making a will

It saves a lot of time and trouble, not to mention distress to family and friends, if a dead person has made a *will* setting out how they want their estate to be distributed. A will is a legal document in which you explain who is to have what when you die. It does not have to be drawn up by a lawyer and there are plenty of DIY kits on the market if you want to save money. But . . . there are two major problems with drawing up your own will:

- What you may think is perfectly clear, unambiguous language may not turn out to be so when the will comes into effect.
- Circumstances may arise to make your home-made will ambiguous or even unenforceable.

A will has to be printed or handwritten, it cannot be recorded on tape or in any other way. The signature of the person making the will (the *testator*) must be witnessed by two people who are not being left anything in it (they are not *beneficiaries*). The language of wills can often seem obscure and non-user-friendly. This is partly because of the urgent need to make sure that they cover every possible eventuality. Some of the specialist words used are listed in the box at the top of the next page.

- **estate**: all the goods, property, and money that the person owns when they die
- **real property/realty**: land and buildings
- **personal property/personalty**: all other possessions
- **bequeath**: the word used to refer to the giving of personal estate
- **devise**: the word used to refer to the giving of real estate
- **residue**: what is left after taxes and funeral expenses have been paid and specific bequests have been made
- **descendants**: the children, and their children, grandchildren, and so on all the way down the line

The executors and probate

The testator appoints one or more people to administer the provisions of the will. These are referred to as *executors* or *personal representatives*. They may be members of the family or personal friends, or possibly a bank or solicitor (who will, of course, charge for their services). When the testator dies the executors are responsible for organising the funeral arrangements and carrying out the provisions of the will. Before this can be done, it is necessary to apply to the Probate Registry for a certificate known as the Grant of Probate. Before doing this it is necessary to make a detailed survey of the estate, listing all the assets and their value, as well as liabilities such as mortgages and bank loans. Items of value such as furniture and paintings have to be valued professionally and stocks and shares must be valued at their price at the time of death. The Inland Revenue must also be informed so that an assessment of tax liability can be made. The list of things to be done goes on and on. It is because there is so much detailed work involved that many executors prefer to engage a solicitor to do it for them. The solicitor's fees will, of course, be deducted from the estate, along with tax and other liabilities before bequests are fulfilled.

Grant of Probate
If there appears to be no challenge to a will, then the Grant of Probate is made 'in common form', after the completion of the relevant formalities by the executors. If there is a later challenge, then this grant can be revoked. In the case of a challenge both sides present their cases in court before a 'solemn form' is granted.

Probate Registry
Probate is granted by the Family Division of the High Court, which operates through local Probate Registries.

5 The law and the householder

CONTENTS

The old saying 'An Englishman's home is his castle' may be a massive over-simplification, but it says something important about the way we feel about the building in which we live. If our enjoyment of our home is threatened from outside, whether that threat comes from a local authority, a mortgage lender, or a 'neighbour from hell', then we feel the attack personally. So the law that governs the ownership and use of property can have a profound influence on our personal lives. But these laws are many and complex. This chapter can only touch on a few. To see which parts of it affect you personally, look at the chart below, which refers you to the relevant page or pages.

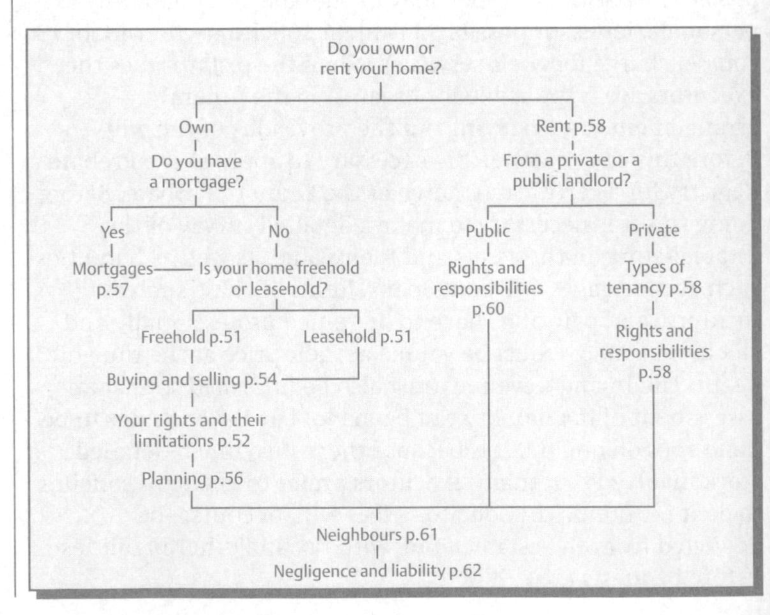

Freehold and leasehold

When you buy a house, you are really buying two things: a piece of land and the building that stands on it. In theory all the land in England belongs to the sovereign and land 'owners' simply have the right to occupy it, but in practice they own it. If you buy a house freehold, then it belongs to you until you decide to dispose of it. When you die, it passes to your heirs. Since you own both the land and the building on it, no one can interfere with either.

In the case of a flat, however, things are more complicated. The land on which a block of flats stands cannot belong to any individual flat, and in addition there are usually parts of the building that belong to everybody (lifts, hallways, and so on). There may also be communal gardens. What is the responsibility of everybody usually ends up being the responsibility of no one. The solution is leasehold: an individual or organization owns the freehold of the land and the block of flats, sells leases to the individuals, and charges them annually for maintaining the communal areas. The flat owners may also have to pay a ground rent. The lease is typically for a long period: 99 years or even 999 years. Of course, as time passes, the length of the lease reduces. It is also possible for houses to be sold leasehold, but this is far less common.

For the period of the lease, the leaseholder has much the same rights as the freeholder, with one or two limitations. In particular, if you wish to make alterations to the property, you may have to get the landlord's consent. This makes sense, since changes made to one flat could well directly affect others in the same block. On the other hand, the restrictions imposed by some landlords can be quite heavy and not necessarily in the leaseholders' own interests. In other countries such as the United States blocks of flats (called 'condominiums') are jointly owned by the owners of the flats, who have responsibility for the communal services. At the time of writing the Government is examining ways of introducing a similar arrangement in England, known as 'commonhold'.

On moving house, the first candidates for the dustbin are your rose-coloured glasses with special hindsight attachment.

Basil Boothroyd, *British humorist*

The owner's rights

So you have bought a house freehold; it's your 'castle', and you can do what you like with it and the land it stands on . . . well, not exactly.

The system of private property is the most important guarantee of freedom.

Friedrich August von Hayek, *economist and Nobel laureate*

Rights

You have the right to enjoy your property without unlawful interference from other people. Other people cannot enter it without your permission, or damage it in any way. If they do, you can sue them for trespass. You can build on it, or pull down buildings that are already there. You can behave on it as you will, without other people stopping you. You can let, sell, bequeath, or give away your property to whomever you please.

But . . .

In practice there are many limitations to those rights. Basically you can enjoy them as long as the law does not limit them in any way. It may also be the case that when you acquired the property there were a number of restrictions built in by the previous owner. For example:

- **Easements**
  Neighbours or the general public may have a right of way across your property. Or a neighbour's drains may cross your land and you cannot interfere with them in any way. Another common easement is when you find that an electricity company has a pole in your garden. You cannot remove it (and you may find that if you ask them to do so they will charge an exorbitant amount).

- **Restrictive covenants**
  When you buy a house, it is quite common to find that there are covenants applying to it restricting your use. They may say, for example, that you can only use it for residential purposes, or that you can't put up a garden shed.

Your rights to enjoy your property are also limited when they come up against the rights of other individuals and those of the community at large. The table below illustrates some of the commonest ways in which this can happen.

Right	Limitations
To destroy buildings	Not if the building is listed.
To construct a new building	May require planning permission and/or building regulations approval. If the proposed new building reduces the amount of light entering that of a neighbour, they may be able to prevent you from building it.
To stop people entering	Not if there is a right of way to individuals or to the public. Under certain circumstances some people have the right to enter (e.g. the police).
To do what you like	Not if it causes a nuisance to others. Not if it is against the law. Not if it infringes local by-laws, Health and Safety Regulations etc.
To dispose of it as you wish	Not if you have a mortgage.

Property is theft.

Pierre-Joseph Proudhon, *19th century French socialist*

Buying and selling

Stages

1 Offer
2 Checking
3 Exchange of contracts
4 Completion

The process by which you transfer the ownership of land from one person to another is called conveyancing. You can do your own conveyancing, but most people use the services of either a solicitor or a licensed conveyancer. The process entails a number of stages; at each of these there are different requirements on buyer and seller (or 'purchaser' and 'vendor').

Preliminary

The seller has to find a buyer and the buyer has to find a house. This is often done through an estate agent, but not always. The house is advertised at an asking price, but this is, of course, only a starting point for negotiations. When the buyer and seller have agreed a price, the house is normally taken off the market.

If you are buying, you then have a lot of work to do before entering into a formal legal agreement to buy. In particular you have to ensure that you know exactly what you are buying and that there are no problems associated with it. You do this by asking the seller a number of questions (usually done by means of a questionnaire supplied by your solicitor), which may, in turn, raise supplementary questions. These range from who is responsible for maintaining garden walls and fences to whether the seller has ever had any disputes with neighbours.

At the same time you need to examine the entry at the Land Registry. This includes a plan showing the boundaries of the property and will tell you who owns it, whether there is a mortgage, and details of covenants which may limit what you can do with the property. You also need to know whether there are any plans to build near the property or drive a road through the middle of it. This is done by asking the local authority for a 'search' of the planning records. Most buyers also arrange to have the property examined by a professional surveyor.

Exchange of contracts

If the answers to all these questions are satisfactory, then buyer and seller are in a position to commit themselves legally to the deal. This is done by drawing up a legal agreement, the contract. This sets out the details of the deal and when it will be concluded ('completion'). Two copies are made and each party signs one. They are then exchanged, so each has proof that the other has signed. At the same time the buyer hands over a deposit (usually between 5% and 10% of the agreed selling price). If the buyer later refuses to go through with the sale, the seller keeps the deposit. If the seller drops out, the buyer can sue for breach of contract, but that is unlikely to provide much satisfaction and may prove expensive.

I have heard of a man who had a mind to sell his house, and therefore carried a piece of brick in his pocket, which he shewed as a pattern to encourage purchasers.

Jonathan Swift, *Anglo-Irish author and satirist*

Before completion

All that remains before completion can take place is for the buyer to draw up the document which will transfer ownership to him or her. This is then approved by the seller. Meanwhile the seller has to ensure that the property is emptied of possessions and rubbish and is fit to be taken over.

Completion

On the appointed day the buyer pays the seller the agreed sum and the seller hands over the signed transfer and the keys to the house.

I want a house that has got over its troubles; I don't want to spend the rest of my life bringing up a young and inexperienced house.

Jerome K. Jerome, *American writer and humourist*

The role of the professional

Not only is the process of conveyancing complicated, there are also important issues of timing: the seller doesn't want to hand over the house until the money is guaranteed and the buyer has similar but opposite concerns. Using a solicitor or licensed conveyancer who can be trusted to hold signed documents and money until the right moment makes the process a lot easier.

Planning

Although the owner of a house has considerable freedom under the law to do with it as they please, there have to be limitations to that freedom. For example, if I change my house from an ordinary dwelling into a late-night fish-and-chip shop, my neighbours will suffer the inconvenience of noise, smells, and litter. Or if I double the size of the house by extending it right up to the road, I not only completely change the nature of the house and street, but I may also create traffic visibility problems.

So local authorities have the power to control 'development', by which is meant: new building; building extensions; and changing the use of a property. If you wish to do any of these things, you have to apply to your district council or unitary authority. In fact it is usually advisable to speak to the planning department about your ideas before making a formal application. They will be able to tell you whether planning consent is necessary and to advise on how to proceed.

You then have to apply for either outline or detailed planning consent. Outline consent means that the council have no objections in principle, but will still need to see the detailed plans before you start work. If you apply for detailed consent you will have to submit detailed plans of the project, which is often expensive. You also have to pay an application fee.

The council will then publicize your proposed development. Usually a notice is put up on site and a copy published in the local paper. The proposal and plans are also available for inspection at the council offices. This is so that other residents have the chance to raise any objections they may have. Objections can only be made on planning grounds, however.

After the period allowed for objections, the application is considered by the planning department, which will then make recommendations to the council's planning committee, and planning consent is then granted or refused.

Even if you do not have to seek planning consent for changes to your house, you may have to apply for building regulations approval. Local authorities administer regulations which control the quality of building work done. So, for example, if you have a built-in garage and wish to convert it into a room, you may not need planning consent but will almost certainly require building regulations approval, because the standard of construction required for a dwelling is higher than that for a garage. Again the local planning department will advise on what is required.

Mortgages

The process of buying a house described on pages 54-55 assumes, of course, that the buyer has the asking price readily available (is a 'cash buyer'). Often that is not the case and the buyer has to borrow some of that money from a bank or building society. To do that you have to take out a mortgage. In everyday language we use the word 'mortgage' to mean a loan we get from a bank or building society to buy a house. Legally what happens is that we get a loan and in return grant a mortgage to the lender, giving them rights over the property. The mortgage is the rights over the property that we sign away, not the money we receive in return.

In effect what you are saying to the lender is 'I will repay this money according to our agreement and if I fail to do so, you can get your money back by selling the house'. The lender then has a 'charge' on the property which is included in the Land Registry entry (i.e. the loan is a matter of public knowledge). The terms of the mortgage are, in fact, a lot tougher than people realize. Once you have signed it, the lender is entitled to take possession of your house whenever they like—they don't have to wait until you fall behind with your repayments. They won't normally do this, but they do place limitations on what you can do with the house. You can't, for example, let it out, or do anything else that may reduce the value of the property (e.g. structural alterations), without their permission—for which, naturally, you will have to pay.

Renting

If you rent a property there are certain issues which are of great importance to you. Very roughly these can be summed up under three headings:

- **Security**
  How easy is it for the landlord to evict you? What rights do you have to stop him or her doing so?

- **Rent**
  How easy is it for the landlord to raise the rent? Do you have any way of stopping or reducing proposed rent rises?

- **Maintenance and repairs**
  Who is responsible for repairs, decorating, and other maintenance?

The answers vary, according to whether your landlord is in the private or public sector.

The private sector

Since 1997 almost all new tenancies have been what are known as *assured shorthold tenancies*. Shorthold tenancies are for a limited period of time during which the tenant is assured of possession, provided they fulfil the terms of their tenancy. At the end of the period of tenancy the landlord can require the tenant to leave. If the tenant does not do so, the landlord has to get a Court Order to enforce the eviction, but does not have to provide any reason other than that the tenancy has ended. In return for these limitations on their security, tenants have some protection against being charged an excessive rent: they can appeal to a Rent Assessment Committee, which may decide that the rent being asked is above the market rent for such premises, and order the landlord to reduce it. There are also restrictions on the way in which a landlord can review and raise the rent.

Greater protection

If your tenancy dates back to before 1977, you are likely to have much greater protection. Essentially your tenancy is likely to be protected and if the landlord wishes to evict you he or she will need to give the Court an explanation of the grounds for this before a Court Order can be obtained. Overall, however, private tenants do not have much security of tenure. They are near the bottom of the 'security ladder'.

Maintenance and repairs

Under the Landlord and Tenant Act 1985, for tenancies lasting less than seven years, the responsibility for repairs lies with the landlord. By 'repairs' is meant essentially replacing or mending things that are broken or worn out—from a flaking ceiling to dangerous out-of-date electrical wiring. This doesn't include improvements such as fitting a new bathroom or installing double glazing. Nor does it cover repairing parts of the structure damaged by the tenant. If you are renting a flat, the landlord's obligation doesn't include repairs to the communal parts of the building unless the landlord owns the whole block. Finally, the Act does not cover decorating the inside of the house or flat. If you have a well-drafted tenancy agreement such matters should be covered, setting out whose responsibility they are.

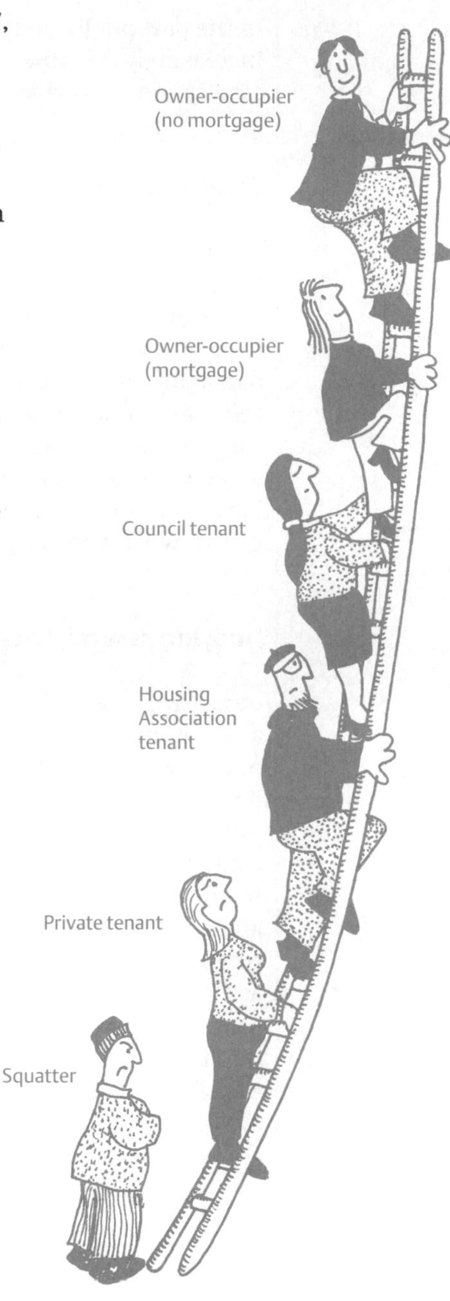

The public sector

Good fences make good neighbours.

Robert Frost, *American poet*

In the past public housing was provided by local authorities. Increasingly this role is being taken over by housing associations of various kinds.

Council tenants

If you are a council tenant you are in a much stronger position than a private tenant. You have a *secure tenancy*, which means that you cannot be evicted unless you give the council grounds for doing so. The grounds include non-payment of rent, damaging the property, anti-social behaviour, and so on. Even then the council must first give notice of this and then go to the Court to obtain a Court Order, which will only be given when the grounds have been proved. On the other hand, you have no protection against rent rises. The council is entitled to charge what it considers to be a reasonable rent.

Housing associations ('Registered Social Landlords')

Increasingly, social housing is provided by housing associations. Since the whole point of this type of housing is to provide good housing for the less well-off, it is a type of housing that favours the tenant. Tenancies are governed by the same laws as private tenancies (which makes them different from council tenancies). They tend to be governed by different sections of those laws than private tenancies, however. The law allows a landlord to grant a tenant an *assured tenancy* with considerable security of tenure, which is what housing associations normally do. There are, technically, no greater limitations on the rent than are available to a shorthold tenant, but housing associations aim to provide affordable housing, so they have clear rules about how much rent can be charged and in what circumstances it can be raised.

Neighbours

Whether you rent or own a flat or a house, you have rights and responsibilities as a householder. Broadly speaking these come under the heads of: nuisance; trespass (technically 'trespass to land'); and negligence.

Nuisance

As we shall see, someone commits trespass if they physically enter your land, but it is possible to interfere with your use and enjoyment of your property without entering it. For example a neighbour may set up a workshop in their back garden and work on noisy machines in the middle of the night, or a nearby householder may decide to keep several pigs on their property. The noise and smell prevent you from enjoying your property in the way you have a right to, and the neighbours are committing a *nuisance*. If the problems persists you have the right to bring an action for nuisance and if you are successful the Court will make an injunction requiring the offender to stop. Such cases are often not clear-cut.

Neighbours from hell.

Trespass

If you own a piece of land, a house or flat, no one else may enter it without your permission. They may not damage it, or put anything on or in it. If they do so, you can either sue them or obtain an injunction from the court banning them from doing so again. Contrary to popular belief, they don't have to have caused any damage for you to exercise your rights. They may argue against this either that they have your permission (for example if you have let the property to them) or that they have a legal right (as may be the case with the police). There may also be rights of way across your land, either to individuals or to the public at large. If you are a tenant you have similar rights to those of an owner-occupier, but these will be limited by your tenancy agreement, which will give the landlord or their representative certain rights of entry.

Negligence

As well as the rights that have been referred to so far, as a householder you also have responsibilities. In particular you have to ensure that your use of your property does not cause injury to other people, whether visiting it or passing nearby. This extends not only to injuries or damage caused because you have failed to maintain your property properly, but also to damage or injuries caused by animals that you have failed to control properly. You are only liable, however, if it can be proved that you were negligent and that the injuries or damage were caused as a direct result of your negligence. The exception to this is in the case of animals that are classified as dangerous. Here the keeper of the animal is liable even if someone else was responsible for allowing the animal out of captivity.

The law and the driver

6

CONTENTS

You are more likely to break the law when driving a car than in any other area of normal life. If you disagree with that statement, just think for a moment: do you never drive at 33 m.p.h. in a built-up area? Never? Have you never been guilty of careless driving? If you were tried and found guilty of either offence you would have committed a crime, as surely as if you went up to your local jeweller's and put a brick through the window in order to steal expensive watches.

But most of us don't look at it in this way. A few m.p.h. over the speed limit, a slightly dodgy bit of overtaking—they don't really feel like crimes, do they? But they are. Motoring offences are tried in exactly the same way as other crimes, and those who are found guilty can be fined thousands of pounds, or sentenced to imprisonment, just as any other criminal. Motoring offences are different, however, in one important respect. A person accused of other crimes has to be shown to have *intended* to commit the act. For example, if you are caught shoplifting it is a reasonable defence to say that you intended to pay for the item but forgot; that you didn't intend to commit an offence. (It may well not work, of course.) No such defence is possible if you are caught speeding. In the case of motoring offences, it is sufficient for the prosecution to prove that you did what you are accused of—whether you meant to or not.

Strict liability
In criminal law this means offences where the prosecution do not have to show *mens rea* (guilty intent). Motoring offences such as speeding come into this category.

What's more, if you are, for example, involved in a traffic accident and are found guilty of driving without due care and attention, other people affected by the accident (an injured pedestrian, for example) can sue you for damages. Indeed, they can do so even if you are not charged or convicted. So the path of the motorist is strewn with hazards. In this chapter we look at the commonest of these and the terminology that is used.

You and your car

'I only borrowed a motor-car while the owners were at lunch; they had no need of it at the time. I didn't mean to steal it, really; but people —especially magistrates— take such harsh views of thoughtless and high-spirited actions.'

Mr Toad in *Wind in the Willows* by Kenneth Grahame

Insurance
In addition to a driving licence you also have to be insured. The minimum requirement is that the driver is insured against injuries caused to other people. Most 'third party, fire, and theft' policies cover rather more than this minimum requirement, and 'fully comprehensive' policies also cover injury to the insured driver and their vehicle.

Even before you turn the key in the ignition, there are a number of legal requirements for both driver and vehicle.

The driver

You must have a licence to drive a car, even as a learner, and before one is issued you have to satisfy a number of requirements: you must be over seventeen years of age; be medically fit to drive; and fulfil the eyesight requirements. People whose medical condition might cause problems while they are in charge of a car (diabetics, for example) can be required to provide a certificate from their GP stating that their condition is under control and not likely to impair their performance as drivers. You cannot, of course, drive a car unsupervised until you have passed the written and practical driving tests, after which you can apply for a full driving licence. This will entitle you to drive a certain range of different vehicle types (there are twenty-two of these). The computerized driving licence system based at Swansea not only records who is allowed to drive what, but also the offences, if any, of which they have been found guilty. Each offence has a code number which is recorded on your licence; at the time of writing there are about sixty of these ranging in seriousness from 'Failure to give information as to identity of driver etc.' to 'Causing death by dangerous driving'.

The car

Like the driver, the vehicle must be licensed. The owner has to pay the road tax, 'vehicle licensing duty' as it is more properly known. Failure to display the tax disc ('road fund licence') is itself an offence. The car also requires a registration document, often referred to as the 'log book'. These are issued at the time of the vehicle's first registration and record changes to the specification of the vehicle and changes of ownership. In addition, if the car has been registered for more than three years, it requires a certificate stating that it has been examined by a registered test station and satisfies the requirements of the Ministry of Transport test (has 'passed its MoT'). A police officer can ask a driver to produce a driving licence, certificate of insurance, and—if applicable—an MoT certificate for the vehicle. If you cannot do so immediately then you will have to do so *in person* within the next seven days at your nearest police station.

Accidents

You will be fortunate indeed if you go through a lifetime's driving without ever being involved in a road traffic accident. Yet many drivers are unclear of what to do when this happens. The comments that follow cover the legal aspects of an accident but not the practical aspects—administering first aid, safety, and so on.

If an accident occurs

Accidents happen very quickly, they can be emotionally disturbing, and their aftermath can be protracted and expensive. So, even in the case of the most minor and apparently harmless accident, drivers have to act prudently to protect their own interests. The advice that is generally given is to say as little as possible (and certainly not to admit it was your fault, or even say sorry, which can be read as admitting liability).

Immediately after an accident, it is important to make as detailed notes as possible of:

- Names and addresses of those involved.
- Details of the vehicles involved, and insurance details.
- Names and addresses of any witnesses.
- What happened, including a sketch plan showing the positions of the vehicles at the time of the accident.

- Time, weather, visibility, road condition.
- Damage caused to vehicles, and any injuries to people.

Unless the accident is very minor, the police should be called, and a note made of the number(s) of the officer(s) attending. Many drivers feel the need to explain what has happened. It is often argued, however, that a driver involved in an accident should not make a statement at this stage, even if asked. Immediately after an accident is not the best time to give a considered statement of something as serious and complex as a vehicle collision. The driver needs time to calm down and reflect on exactly what happened.

Keeping a record
In these days of disposable cameras, some drivers keep one in the car, so that they can make an exact record in the event of an accident.

'Say cheese!'

Action to be taken later

Drivers who belong to a motoring organization, or have an insurance policy which offers legal advice, can contact them and inform them that they have been involved in accident.

When they get home, drivers are advised to:

- get any injuries, however slight, checked out by a doctor;
- report the accident to their insurers by phone;
- make a detailed written description of what happened, with a sketch plan.

There is no juridical distinction between fire-arms, wild beasts, and motor cars where the safety and peace of the King's highway are concerned.

A. P. Herbert, *British writer, lawyer, and politician*

Criminal and civil law

A momentary lapse of attention, driving too close to the vehicle in front, a slight excess of speed, and two vehicles collide. When a road traffic accident occurs, it is usually someone's fault—more often than not the fault of one or more of the drivers or pedestrians involved. What happens next may involve criminal law, or civil law, or both.

If the police believe that any one of the sixty-odd motoring offences has been committed *and that there is a good chance of gaining a conviction* then they (or rather the Crown Prosecution Service) may decide to prosecute. The main headings under which a driver may be charged are these:

- **Careless driving**
  The best known of these is 'Driving without due care and attention', and it is an offence which most drivers have been guilty of at one time or another in their careers. If every offence were prosecuted, the Magistrates' Courts would be clogged up. Prosecutions normally follow either an accident or the observation by a police officer of a particularly stupid piece of driving. If found guilty you are liable to a fine and to having your licence endorsed.

- **Dangerous driving**
  It is difficult to pin down when careless driving shades into dangerous driving, but the more serious offence is characterized by a deliberate disregard for other road users and actions which are likely to cause (or have caused) danger to others. Drivers charged with dangerous driving are usually charged with careless driving as well—as a kind of insurance policy for police and prosecution. If you are found guilty of dangerous driving you can be sent to prison as well as losing your licence.

  If someone is killed as a result of your dangerous driving, you can be charged with manslaughter. In the past juries were reluctant to convict in such cases, so a separate offence was introduced of causing death by dangerous driving. Those found guilty are commonly sent to prison and disqualified.

Do you know?
Apart from licence endorsements, what is the maximum penalty for each of the following traffic offences?

1. Failing to stop after an accident
2. Driving without insurance
3. Driving without wearing a seatbelt
4. Taking a vehicle without the owner's consent

Answers on next page.

Answers to 'Do you know?'
At the time of writing these were:

1 £5,000
2 £1,000
3 £500
4 £5,000

Drink or drugs

Unlike charges of careless or dangerous driving, which require the court to come to a decision based on their opinion of the circumstances, the charge of 'Driving or attempting to drive with alcohol level above the permitted limit' is largely a question of scientific evidence. A specimen is taken and analysed and if it shows that the driver has exceeded the permitted level of alcohol or has driven under the influence of drugs, then there is no defence and a court will deliver a guilty verdict. This leads to automatic disqualification and a fine, with almost no exceptions. There are related charges including being 'in charge of a vehicle while unfit through drink' and similar charges for those who have taken drugs.

Speed limits

This, too, is largely a matter of scientific evidence, provided usually by a speed camera or a radar gun. Of course, a camera only produces evidence of the car, not the driver. The police then contact the registered owner of the vehicle and if he or she was not driving at the time they are required to state who was. Normally if you were driving at up to 25 m.p.h. above the limit you will face a fixed penalty. If you were doing a higher speed (i.e. more than 25 m.p.h. above the limit) you will face a court case. The maximum penalty for speeding is a fine of £1,000 and disqualification, but most offenders receive a lower fine and their licences are endorsed.

Traffic direction and signs

There are a number of offences under this heading, including 'Failing to comply with traffic light signals' and 'Failing to comply with double white lines', both of which will usually result in a fine and a licence endorsement.

Vehicle and documentation

If you drive without a licence or insurance, or while disqualified, then you can be fined or even (in the case of driving while disqualified) imprisoned. If you drive a vehicle that is defective, you can be fined up to £2,500.

What happens if you are charged

For most motoring offences, the offender is sent a summons by post, detailing the charge(s) to be brought. This will either state when and where you are to appear for trial or offer the opportunity to plead guilty by post. (It is not possible to plead not guilty by post, for obvious reasons.) The vast majority of motoring cases are heard in Magistrates' Courts, but some, usually the more serious, are tried in the Crown Court. For offences in the middle range of seriousness the defendant can opt for a Crown Court trial before a jury; people believe with some justice that since juries tend to be composed mainly of motorists they are more likely to be sympathetic than a panel of magistrates. This right is, however, under attack from the Government, since jury cases are longer and more expensive.

The roles of the different courts are described in chapter 3 on pages 26–27.

Civil liability

Even if no one is charged after an accident, it is usually the case that damage has been done and that someone will have to pay for it to be repaired. Often what happens is that those involved make a claim under their insurance policies. The problem here is that if you do so, you risk losing your no claim bonus, which may mean paying hundreds of pounds in extra premiums.

The alternative is to make a claim directly against the other person(s) whom you consider to be responsible for the accident. As a driver you have a responsibility to behave reasonably and in such a way as to avoid harming others. In other words you should obey all the rules and follow the Highway Code. If you do not, and an accident occurs, then you have been negligent. Anyone injured or suffering a loss as a result of a driver's negligence can sue them for damages. So if you can demonstrate that the other motorist was wholly to blame, you can claim full compensation from them (or their insurers). In many instances, however, it is not so clear cut. The blame may be shared between two or more drivers. In this case, unless you want to be involved in protracted litigation, you will probably have to settle for a 50/50 division of blame, and lose part or all of your no claim bonus.

7 The world of work

CONTENTS

This chapter is mainly concerned with the rights and obligations of employers and employees. It concludes with a short section about working for yourself. As those who are self-employed will know, they have far fewer statutory rights than employees, and their relationships with those they work for are governed by the contracts they enter into. So, for example, as a freelance author I have a contract with the publisher which governs such things as the length of this book, when I have to deliver the final manuscript, and how (and how much) I shall be paid. If a dispute arises, the contract sets out how it is to be resolved; in the last resort one party might have to sue the other for breach of contract. In the world of employers and employees, by contrast, there are both statutory controls and agreed procedures governing their behaviour.

The contract of employment

I have long been of the opinion that if work were such a splendid thing the rich would have kept more of it for themselves.

Bruce Grocott, *British Labour Party Member of Parliament*

Every employer is required by law to provide every employee with a statement of the main terms and conditions of their employment within two months of their starting work. This has to contain details of the job, rates and methods of payment, the hours to be worked, holidays, disciplinary procedures, and so on. It is not the same as the contract of employment, which may, in fact, never be written down. But even if it is not written down, it still exists: once the post has been offered and accepted and the employer has agreed to pay the employee, there is a contract. If either then says, 'I've changed my mind', they are in breach of contract. If the employer, for example, withdrew the job offer, the employee could sue for wrongful dismissal—even though nothing existed on paper.

Implied terms

The job description, rates and methods of payment, and other specific details form the express terms of the contract of employment. As well as these express terms, the contract has a range of 'implied terms'. These come from the common law and from statutes enacted by Parliament.

There is more about implied terms in chapter 2 on page 19, and in the Glossary.

Common law implied terms

These include such things as:

- the employee will show the competence needed to do the job properly;
- the employee will obey reasonable orders and instructions;
- the employee will work for the employer in good faith and not, for example, secretly do competing work for a rival company;
- the employer will provide a safe working environment (although this is also covered by a range of statutory requirements).

Statutory implied terms

These include:

- health and safety;
- freedom from discrimination (on grounds of gender, race / ethnicity, marital status, or disability);
- equal pay for men and women;
- patents and copyright (provisions that if an employee invents or creates something as part of their work, the rights in it belong to the company and not to the individual creator).

Discipline

It's true hard work never killed anybody, but I figure why take the chance?

Ronald Reagan, *US President*

One of the things that a written contract has to contain is a description of the disciplinary procedure within the company. If you work for somebody you need to know:

- whom you are responsible to;
- what you have to do if you have a grievance;
- what will happen if you fail in your work:
  - how your case will be handled,
  - how you can defend yourself,
  - who you can appeal to if you think you have been unfairly treated.

The main guidelines that employers follow are contained in the Code of Conduct drawn up by the Advisory, Conciliation, and Arbitration Service (ACAS). This sets out a framework within which employers should establish their own detailed rules and procedures. It recommends that all employees should be given a document explaining the rules and procedures when they start work. The ACAS Code is not mandatory and indeed it is not followed by all employers, but those who do not follow it may find that they have to justify this if they are ever called before an Employment Tribunal.

The Code maps out a route for handling disciplinary problems. At each stage, it should be made clear in writing to the employee not only the nature of the offence, but also how and by whom it is to be handled. There are four stages:

1 **Oral warning**
This is done formally and followed by a written confirmation.

2 **First written warning**
If the behaviour that has been complained about continues, the employee is given a written warning, detailing the offence and setting out the possibility that they may be dismissed if it is repeated.

3 **Final written warning**
If the offence is repeated, the employee is warned that any further repetition will lead to their dismissal.

4 **Dismissal**

Dismissal

There are three main grounds on which an employer can dismiss an employee:

- Capacity
- Conduct
- Redundancy

Capacity

If the employee proves to be incapable of doing the job for which they are employed, then they may be dismissed. For example if you lie at interview about academic qualifications or training that are required for the job, when your employer finds out about it they may reasonably dismiss you. By the same token if a certain job demands certain skills and the employee knows this and fails to reach the required standards, then they can be dismissed. It may also happen that a person becomes incapable of doing their job through ill-health. If it is unlikely that they will recover sufficiently to be able to do that job again, or it is likely that after recovering the same problem will recur, then the employer may reasonably dismiss the employee. In all these cases, however, the employer has to act fairly, discussing the problem with the employee and going through a process similar to that outlined above. Employees should be given the chance of improving and should be offered, where appropriate, opportunities for training or, failing that, suitable alternative employment within the company where this is available. It is only when all these options have been exhausted that the employee may fairly be dismissed.

A professional is a man who can do his job when he doesn't feel like it. An amateur is a man who can't do his job when he does feel like it.

James Agate, *British critic and essayist*

Acting fairly
Employers have to take existing employment law into account when considering dismissing an employee. For example an employer who dismisses a worker on grounds of ill-health may fall foul of the Disability Discrimination Act.

Conduct

Employees can be dismissed because of the way they have behaved, or misbehaved. The two types of misconduct are treated in different ways.

- **Gross misconduct**
  Certain actions are so serious that an employee can be sacked out of hand—no warnings, no period of notice to be worked, no further payment. But the behaviour has to be very serious. It includes:

  - serious negligence
  - serious insubordination
  - refusal to carry out reasonable instructions
  - sexual harassment
  - fraud
  - theft
  - violence
  - abusing alcohol at work

The definition and consequences of gross misconduct are often included in a contract of employment.

- **Ordinary misconduct**
  Other actions are less serious. For example:
  - failure to carry out reasonable instructions
  - problems of attitude or relationships with other workers
  - continually being late for work

For this type of behavioural problem, it is necessary for the employer to go through the full disciplinary procedure outlined on pages 72–73. At each stage employees have to be given the opportunity to explain themselves and the chance to show that they can improve. If in the end they are dismissed then they must be given the full period of notice specified in their contract (or payment in lieu).

Redundancy

The other major way in which an employee may be dismissed is through redundancy. A new employee is appointed to a defined position within an organization. Circumstances may change so that the work done by the person filling that post is no longer needed. In that situation the post (not the person) becomes redundant and the person filling it is dismissed. Typically this can happen because:

- the business or part of it is closing down;
- changes to the firm's economic or financial situation mean that it has to reduce its workforce;
- restructuring within the organization means that departments and their requirements change.

Employment law requires employers to treat employees who are made redundant fairly. The main requirements are as follows:

1. The provisions for statutory redundancy payments apply to anyone who has worked for a company full-time for at least two years and is then made redundant.
2. Employees should in the first instance be offered 'suitable' alternative employment.
3. 'Suitable' means, roughly speaking, work that is of a comparable status and pay (and other terms) and which is within reasonable geographical reach for the employee.
4. If the person concerned turns down such an offer 'unreasonably' then they are not eligible for compensation.
5. If suitable alternative employment is unavailable, then redundancy payment must be offered.
6. The amount of statutory redundancy payment will depend on age, length of service, and rate of pay. It can range from one week's pay to thirty weeks', with a maximum payment, which at the time of writing was £7,200.

In the end we are all sacked and it's always awful. It is as inevitable as death following life. If you are elevated there comes a day when you are demoted. Even Prime Ministers.

Alan Clark, *Conservative Minister, writing of ministerial office in his diary*

Contractual redundancy payment
Employers may, of course, offer employees payments that are higher than the statutory amounts listed in the text.

7 Employers have to demonstrate fairness in handling redundancy. To do this they must consult the workforce, either through recognized trade unions or, if none are recognized, through representatives of the workforce.
8 Employers must also show fairness in the ways in which they select those who are to be made redundant.
9 The redundancy has to be genuine; you cannot make a post redundant as a convenient way of getting rid of a troublesome employee and then employ someone else to do the same work. Such an action would be unfair dismissal.
10 If the employer fails to act fairly, then the way may be open to workers to claim unfair dismissal (and the consequent possibility of higher compensation payments, since Tribunals can make much higher awards in certain circumstances).

Feeling redundant again.

Unfair dismissal

If employees feel that their employer has behaved unfairly in dismissing them, especially if they have not gone through the proper procedures, they are entitle to claim unfair dismissal and apply to have their case heard by an Employment Tribunal. They can apply to be reinstated or to be paid compensation. They can also apply to the Tribunal if their employer has behaved so unreasonably as to force them to resign. This is known as 'constructive dismissal'.

If the Employment Tribunal finds that the employee's case is justified then they can require the employer to take them back. If this is not practicable or reasonable, then the employee will be awarded compensation. The size of the basic award will depend on the employee's age, length of service, and salary, but the Tribunal may also grant a compensatory award, to compensate the employee for loss of prospects, future salary, and so on. If the Tribunal requires the employer to take the employee back and the employer refuses, the Tribunal can grant an additional award as well as the basic and compensatory awards.

Wrongful dismissal

It is important to remember that unfair dismissal is different from wrongful dismissal. You are wrongfully dismissed if the employer fails to carry out the terms of your contract, typically by failing to give you the specified period of notice or payment in lieu. Here your redress may be to go to the Employment Tribunal, but you could also go to the County Court as with other cases of breach of contract. Of course, an employee can also be in breach of their contract if they leave their job without giving the specified period of notice. It is, however, rare for employers to take such cases to court, for obvious reasons. Usually the most the employee risks is damage to their prospect of future employment, since they cannot easily refer to their most recent employer when applying for a new job.

Web site
Useful information about unfair dismissal can be found at:
www.compactlaw.co.uk/monster/empf1.html

Tribunal Awards

Basic
Based on age, service, salary—up to a maximum of £7,800*

Compensatory
To cover loss of future earnings and prospect—up to a maximum of £53,500*

Additional
If the employer refuses to reinstate—up to a maximum of £13,520*

*These figures are for 2003. The amounts are upgraded annually.

Health and safety

Employers have both common law and statutory obligations to ensure their workers' health and safety.

Common law

Under common law employers have a duty of care towards those who work for them. This requires that they provide:

- a safe place in which to work, and safe access to it;
- safe tools, equipment, materials, and processes;
- where relevant, safe fellow-workers who know what they are doing.

Statutes

A number of statutes relate to health and safety at work, including:

- the Health & Safety at Work Act 1974
- the Workplace Health & Safety & Welfare Regulations 1992

What is entailed

The various regulations cover a large number of issues and are, as might be expected, detailed and wide-ranging. Among other things they cover:

- Accidents
- Fire
- Dangerous substances

- Machinery and safety equipment
- Noise
- Employees' responsibilities
- VDUs

These laws and regulations are enforced by the Health and Safety Executive.

Working hours

A number of regulations concern working hours, breaks, and holidays:

- **48-hour week**
  With certain exceptions workers should not be required to work for more than an average of 48 hours per week.
- **4 weeks' holiday**
  Similarly most workers are entitled to 4 weeks' paid holiday each year. This includes, however, the 8 public holidays in the year and if employers stick to the minimum requirement, workers only receive just over two weeks' holiday in addition (since a week = 5 working days).

  Some categories of workers are excluded from this provision. They include the police, the armed forces, and those working in transport and in the fishing industry.
- **Rest breaks**
  There are also regulations governing breaks and periods of continuous working. Adult workers are entitled to 11 hours' rest in every twenty-four, plus 24 hours in every seven days (or 48 hours in every two-week period). Workers aged sixteen to eighteen are entitled to more generous rest breaks.
- **Night working**
  There are also regulations governing the maximum number of hours to be worked at night.

Working for yourself

Increasing numbers of people are working for themselves rather than being employed. It is impossible in a short space to cover all the legal implications of self-employment and anyone contemplating it should read a specialist book on the subject and take professional advice. What follows is a brief outline of some of the issues.

Legal status
When you run your own business, your legal status has important effects on, among other things:

- your rights and duties as a worker
- your position if you employ staff
- how (and how much) finance can be raised
- your position if you get into debt
- your tax liability.

Legal status

If you work for yourself you have to choose what your legal status should be. You can choose to be a sole trader, or you can work with others either in a partnership or by forming a company.

Sole trader

As a sole trader you take full responsibility for your business. There are no legal formalities before you begin; you just start work. You are solely responsible for the finances of your enterprise; you are personally liable for debts incurred and if your creditors take you to court for non-payment, the court can send the bailiffs in to seize your property. Equally of course, after the Inland Revenue have taken their cut, all the profits belong to you.

Sole traders have to establish with the Revenue that they are genuinely self-employed. The authorities are applying increasing pressure to make as many people as possible employed rather than self-employed, since the self-employed are able to claim many more expenses against tax. If your turnover exceeds a certain amount (£55,000 per annum at the time of writing), you must also register with HM Customs and Excise for Value Added Tax. You then have to charge your customers VAT, adding, at the time of writing, 17.5% to your prices. When you purchase goods and services you can reclaim any VAT paid.

Partnership

If two or more self-employed people work together they can set up a partnership. This doesn't require any legal preliminaries, although many choose to draw up a legal agreement defining the partnership and establishing the share of the profits each partner is entitled to. Such agreements usually also establish procedures for settling disputes and breaking up the partnership.

The assets of a partnership are jointly owned by the partners, who are all individually responsible for the partnership's debts. All business expenditure and VAT payments are deducted from income before the partners receive their shares, which are then taxed as income (after personal and other allowances) in the normal way.

Limited company

A limited company is set up by two or more people, each of whom pays a share of the start-up capital (which may be as little as £1 each). There are set rules on how limited companies have to be established and run, and these are the responsibility of Companies House in Cardiff.

A limited company is a legal entity, which means that it exists apart from the individuals who own it or who are employed by it. If the company fails and becomes bankrupt, the shareholders are not personally liable for all the debts; their liability is limited to the value of the shares they hold. This is clearly an advantage, but it is often negated because banks offering credit may require the shareholders to offer personal guarantees (for example they may have to offer the security of their own homes).

If you set up a limited company you can receive income from it in two ways: as dividends on your shares and as a salary as an employee of the company. In effect the money is taxable twice: the company's profits are liable for corporation tax and both dividends and salaries are liable for income tax.

8 Money and shopping

CONTENTS

Buying goods

When you buy something from a shop, at a market, by phone, or on the Internet you are entering into a contract with the seller. For your part you are agreeing to pay the price asked by the trader (so if, for example, you pay with a cheque that bounces, you have broken your part of the contract). The trader is responsible for ensuring that the goods you are buying are satisfactory.

The main items of legislation which govern this relationship are:

There is more about contracts in chapter 2 on pages 17-20.

- **Sale of Goods Act 1979**
- **Sale and Supply of Goods (Amendment) Act 1994**

If you find that goods you have bought are faulty in some way, you have two possible remedies: via the manufacturer's guarantee (if there is one), or via the retailer's (seller's) liability.

The seller's liability

If goods are faulty it is the seller who is liable, not the manufacturer. The seller must ensure that the goods are:

- **Accurately described**
  So if, for example, the description on the box says that a new computer comes with software X ready installed, and it hasn't, then you can complain.

- **Of satisfactory quality**
  This phrase replaces the older term 'of merchantable quality'. The 1994 act explains that 'satisfactory quality' covers such things as surface appearance, absence of defects, and safety.

- **Fit for their purpose**
  This means 'fit for the purpose for which such goods are normally used'. If the seller has told you that the goods are suitable for a particular purpose (for example in response to an enquiry) then they must be fit for that purpose.

The buyer's remedies

What you can get back if goods are faulty depends on the speed with which you make a claim. The law allows you a reasonable time in which to assess the goods. If you buy a car, for example, you cannot reasonably be expected to assess it on the forecourt; you need to take it home and drive it for a while. You can't on the other hand, drive it for a year and then reasonably complain that it has a fault. After that period of time you would be seen to have accepted the goods and the contract would be valid. If you reject the goods as faulty within a reasonable period of time, then you are entitled to a full refund. The seller may offer a credit note, or replacement item, or a free repair, but you don't have to accept this unless you want to. These rights apply to sale and second-hand goods as well as to new ones, although in the case of second-hand items the definition of 'satisfactory quality' would take the age of the goods into account.

European Directive
The period of time within which a purchaser may complain about faulty goods will be defined by a new European Consumer Guarantees Directive, which is, at the time of writing, awaiting incorporation into UK law. This asserts that if a fault appears in the six months after purchase it can be assumed that it was there from the start and the burden is on the seller to prove that this is not the case. It also defines the purchaser's rights in the event of a defect appearing in the first two years of a product's life.

Private sales

If you buy goods privately—for example a second-hand car being sold by the present owner—then most of the rights described so far do not apply. The seller must still not misrepresent the goods to you by telling you things about them that are not true. Beyond that the principle of the law is summed up in the old Latin tag *caveat emptor*: let the buyer beware!

Buying services

Advertising may be described as the science of arresting human intelligence long enough to get money from it.

Stephen Leacock, *political economist and humorist*

When you purchase services rather than goods the rules are rather different. You are still entering into a contract with the provider, but the way in which this works depends to some extent on the service. The main problem with services is that they are more difficult to pin down than goods. Also they tend to go on over a period of time, which may make it difficult to know exactly when to intervene when things start going wrong. If, for example, you are having building work done on your house, you may not wish to keep nagging the builder over small defects; if you leave things too long, however, the builder may argue that you should have pointed them out at the time.

The key to this is to ensure that when you are having some work done you have a written agreement setting out:

- the dates when work is to start and finish;
- detailed prices;
- the quality of workmanship;
- aftercare—cleaning up and making good defects.

Many service providers, such as large garages, will do this by means of a standard form that the customer signs before work begins. If so, you should, of course, make sure that you read it carefully before signing.

Implied terms

There is more about express and implied terms in chapter 2 on page 19.

As with other contracts, your agreement with a service provider consists of both express and implied terms. The implied terms cover such things as:

- the work should be done with reasonable care and skill;
- it should be done within a reasonable time and for a reasonable price (where these are not specified in a written contract).

Trade descriptions

As we have seen, the description of goods and services forms part of the agreement between seller and customer; if the description is misleading then the customer may be able to claim damages. Descriptions are also covered by the criminal law. The 1968 Trade Descriptions Act makes it an offence to issue a false or misleading description of goods or services. In the case of goods it is enough for the seller to have made a false or misleading description; with services the misdescription has to be knowing or reckless.

The Act does not cover advertising, which is subject to a voluntary trade watchdog, the Advertising Standards Authority, to whom you should address complaints about advertisements. If this fails to resolve a problem, then the Director General of the Office of Fair Trading is empowered to act. There are also regulations about the display of prices. Pre-packaged goods (for example foods) have to have a clearly-displayed price. It is also required that hotels, restaurants, and theatres display their prices. (Also, if a restaurant includes a compulsory service charge it has to announce this fact near the entrance, otherwise you can refuse to pay it.) On one hand, if a shop displays goods that are mistakenly-priced, they are not obliged to sell them to you at that price—or, indeed, at all. The displayed price is simply an 'offer to treat'. On the other hand, if you agree to buy at the displayed price and pay a deposit, then the shop cannot later refuse to sell, because you have entered into an agreement—unless they can prove that you (the buyer) must have known that the price was wrong.

Holidays
If you buy a package holiday your contract is with the tour operator rather than the travel agent from whom you buy the holiday. If they fail to provide the holiday you think you have paid for, then they may be in breach of contract. The contract consists of express and implied terms. The express terms are contained in the terms and conditions printed on the booking form, the holiday details in the brochure, and any additional features you have requested in the booking form. If things go wrong, it is important to complain promptly. If you wait until the holiday is over and you are back home, it could be argued that you have enjoyed the holiday and are now just trying to get some of your money back.

Buying goods on the internet

In theory if you buy goods from the web site of a company based in England you have the same rights as if you had gone into a shop. In practice it may be difficult to track down who is responsible if things go wrong. If you buy from a company based overseas, the law governing the purchase is that of the country in which the company is based—and it may be even more difficult to get redress if things go wrong.

The small print

This contract is so one-sided that I am astonished to find it written on both sides of the paper.

Lord Evershed, *former Master of the Rolls on a standard form contract*

Most of us have at one time or another been asked to sign an agreement on the back of which is a mass of 'Terms and Conditions' . . . and most of us have signed without bothering to read all that small print. It is unfortunately the case that if we do that we may find that we have limited our rights in ways of which we are unaware. It is essential to read the words to which you are putting your name.

But while a seller's terms and conditions may limit our rights, they cannot take away rights to which we are entitled by statute or common law. The Unfair Contract Terms Act 1977 says that, among other things, the 'small print' cannot take away rights that the consumer has under the Sale of Goods Act. These rights were enhanced in 1999 by the Unfair Terms in Consumer Contracts Regulations. Under these, not only can an individual seek redress if a consumer contract is unfair, but also a variety of governmental and non-governmental organizations have the right to do so. (The Office of Fair Trading itself has an Unfair Contract Terms Unit which investigates cases.) These Regulations say that if printed standard business contracts contain 'unfair' terms they cannot be used to deprive consumers of their right to redress. What is

'This is our standard contract. Before you sign it make sure you read the small print.'

meant by 'unfair' is something for a court to decide, but unfair terms would include provisions that penalize the consumer too heavily for failure to pay (or repay) within a given period, or which make it difficult to pay the full amount due ahead of time.

Manufacturers' liability

Manufacturers have a responsibility to ensure that goods are not faulty or dangerous. If an electrical product, for example, is faulty and causes a fire which damages a person's property, then they can sue the manufacturer for damages. This is one of the reasons why manufacturers and retailers make every effort to recall goods as soon as it is suspected that they may be faulty in any way.

Copyright

It might seem reasonable to assume that once you have bought a product you are free to use it in any way you wish. This is not the case and there are many restrictions on what you can do with your purchases. One of the most important of these is the law of copyright.

If you buy a book, or anything else printed, a CD or CD-ROM, a video or DVD, you are entitled to use them for your own enjoyment. But you are not entitled to broadcast them to others or to copy and distribute them without permission. This is because the rights of the creator(s) are protected by copyright law, in particular the Copyright, Designs, and Patents Act 1988. So, for example, if you photocopy this book you are infringing my rights as author, and those of Oxford University Press as publisher. (And if you look on page 4 you will see a statement to this effect.) Certain limited copying is allowed for private study purposes. In addition many institutions, organizations, and businesses pay for a licence to make copies for educational and business purposes, but the amounts that can be copied are strictly controlled. There are similar restrictions on the copying of music, videos, and computer software.

9 Human rights

CONTENTS

A government that is above the law is a menace to be defeated.

Lord Scarman, *Judge and Lord of Appeal*

Until relatively recently human rights in England were bedevilled by the fact that we have no written constitution and that since Britain is a monarchy, its people are subjects rather than citizens. Membership of the European Union changed that. Issues of human rights began to be referred to the European Court of Human Rights and then, in 1998, the Human Rights Act incorporated the European Convention on Human Rights into UK law. For the first time British citizens of the European Union had basic civil liberties enshrined in their own national law.

The Human Rights Act

The Act defines a number of basic rights:

- Right to life
- Freedom from torture
- Freedom from slavery and forced labour
- Right to liberty and security
- Right to a fair trial
- Freedom from punishment except under the law
- Right to respect for private and family life
- Freedom of thought, conscience, and religion
- Freedom of expression
- Freedom of assembly and association

- Right peacefully to enjoy property
- Right to education
- Right to free, secret elections

Any 'public authority' which acts so as to conflict with these rights is behaving unlawfully. This includes courts, which have a duty to interpret existing laws in such a way that they are compatible with the principles of the Convention on Human Rights. In extreme cases the courts may have to declare that a particular law is incompatible with the Convention. If this happens, the government is required to review the law and make necessary amendments. If individuals consider that their rights under the Act have been violated they may take their case to the courts. If a court then finds that the principles of the Convention have been broken it can act to remedy the abuse.

Parliament itself would not exist in its present form had people not defied the law.

Arthur Scargill, *President of the National Union of Miners*

There are, needless to say, numerous qualifications to the rights listed above. Some are obvious. If a person commits a crime, then their right to liberty may have to be curtailed. The right to freedom of expression is limited by the law of defamation, and so on. Some lawyers have argued that the Human Rights Act is too conservative, but most agree, at the time of writing, that it is too early to assess its impact.

Exercising their right to freedom of expression.

You and the police

Men are not hanged for stealing horses, but that horses may not be stolen.

George Savile, Marquis of Halifax (1633–95)

One of the ways in which our freedom is limited is in our relations with the police. Society has created laws to protect the rights and freedoms of individuals and empowered the police to enforce those laws. The police have been given certain powers to enable them to do this: they can ask for information from us and, under certain circumstances, they can arrest us.

Arrest

If the police arrest someone they forcibly detain them against their will. Traditionally the police applied to a magistrate for a warrant before making an arrest. Although this is still possible, they now have wide powers of arrest without the need for a warrant. If they find a person committing an arrestable offence, or believe that they have done so, they can arrest them.

Citizen's arrest
The right to arrest is not confined to police officers. Any citizen can make an arrest if they reasonably believe that another person has committed, or is committing an arrestable offence. If, however, they get it wrong and no offence has been committed or the arrested person is not the guilty party, then they can be sued for false imprisonment.

Arrestable offence

Arrestable offences are those which:

- carry a fixed sentence (e.g. murder); or
- carry a maximum sentence of five years' imprisonment or more; or
- have been made arrestable offences by Parliament.

There are a number of other situations in which the police can arrest people without a warrant, including breach of the peace, driving while disqualified, and disorderly conduct.

The procedure

When the police arrest someone, they have to tell them why (the offence) and they have to caution them.

The caution

You do not have to say anything. But it may harm your defence if you do not mention when questioned something which you later rely on in court. Anything you do say may be given in evidence.

The suspect is then taken to the police station, where they have other rights:

- to see a solicitor
- to inform a family member or friend.

(These rights may be withheld in certain clearly-defined circumstances.)

Before suspects are interviewed they have to be cautioned again. The effect of the wording of the caution is to make it more difficult to remain silent with impunity. On the other hand many lawyers advise that you should not say anything until a solicitor has had the chance to advise you.

After arresting a suspect, the police cannot hold them for an unlimited time without formally charging them. Except in cases where a 'serious' offence has been committed, the person can only be detained for twenty-four hours. They then have to be charged or released. In the case of a 'serious' offence a senior officer can order an initial thirty-six hours' detention and further periods up to ninety-six hours without charge can be authorized by a Magistrates' Court.

If you want to know who your friends are, get yourself a jail sentence.

Charles Bukowski, *American poet and novelist*

Helping with enquiries

There are also many situations in which police wish to question someone without (or before) arresting them. If you have not been arrested, you are not obliged to assist the police in any way (although you may feel that you have a civic or moral duty to do so). The police may ask you to go to the police station for questioning. You don't have to go, nor can they keep you there, unless they arrest you.

Freedom from discrimination

Ageism
The Government announced in June 2003 that it proposed to introduce new legislation on discrimination. This would make it illegal to discriminate in the workplace against an individual on grounds of their age.

An important human right is that all members of society should be treated equally and should be able to take action against those who refuse to do this. It is illegal to discriminate against people in important areas of life on grounds of:

- race
- sex
- disability.

The Race Relations Act

This act, passed in 1976 and later amended, makes it an offence to discriminate against a person on grounds of race, nationality, or ethnic origin. It covers discrimination in the following areas:

- employment and training
- education
- housing
- provision of goods and services.

The act covers three different types of discrimination: direct discrimination, indirect discrimination, and victimization. Indirect discrimination occurs when a person behaves in a way that is not overtly racist but which has racist results. For example if employers say that all male staff must be clean-shaven they are discriminating against Sikhs. Victimization covers such acts as picking on an employee because of their race.

The act also makes it a criminal offence to incite racial hatred whether personally or in the media. Racial harassment and abuse are also criminal offences.

The Sex Discrimination Act

The act prohibits discrimination on grounds of sex (regardless of age) in the same areas as the Race Relations Act (employment and training, education, housing, provision of goods and services). It also forbids discrimination against married people in the area of employment. It refers to both direct and indirect discrimination. An example of indirect discrimination would be if a school ran a lunch-time crafts club which was only open to pupils studying for a technology exam course where almost all those exam candidates were boys.

There are a number of exceptions, many of them obvious and common sense. For example some jobs require a man or woman on grounds of decency (as in some areas of medicine), or practicality (e.g. the role of a woman in a play would normally be given to a woman). In education, too, there are exceptions: single sex schools are allowed, for example. Similarly since the physical strengths of men and women are different, it is not illegal to have separate athletics events for men and women.

The Disability Discrimination Act

This act was passed in 1995 and at the time of writing its provisions are still being implemented. The act differs from those relating to race and sex because it does not attempt to set down a general principle of equality. Instead it defines areas where discrimination on grounds of disability is not allowed.

The act defines a disabled person as 'anyone with a physical or mental impairment which has substantial and long-term adverse effect upon their ability to carry out normal day-to-day activities'. It covers discrimination against disabled people in the areas of housing, employment, education, transport, and the provision of goods and services. A number of physical and psychological conditions are excluded from the disability definition, including addiction to drugs, alcohol, and tobacco.

Freedom of expression

The Human Rights Act says that 'Everyone has the right of freedom of expression,' but that 'the exercise of these freedoms . . . may be subject to such . . . restrictions or penalties as are prescribed by the law.' This includes such restrictions as national security, confidentiality, and protecting the reputations and rights of others.

So it is a question of balance. It would seem unreasonable to argue that in a free society freedom of expression should extend to the publication of top secret government documents. On the other hand, British government ministers and civil servants are among the most secretive in the world, seeking to keep secret many things that in other countries are freely available. Prosecutions under the Official Secrets Act are, however, less common than cases of defamation.

Defamation

Love your enemy. It will ruin his reputation.

Archbishop Desmond Tutu

If you make public a statement that damages someone's reputation, that person may sue you for defamation. You have harmed them personally and they may require recompense in the form of damages; they will also want the truth made public.

Defamation comes in two forms:

- **Libel**
  This is when the defamatory statement is published in a permanent form, such as a newspaper or book, film, or TV broadcast. For libel there is no need for the claimant to prove that they have suffered any material or financial damage.

- **Slander**
  If the defamatory statement is made in a temporary form, usually speech, then it is slander, and the claimant has to prove that they have suffered material or financial damage. Slander is regarded as less serious because it is less

permanent and, in the nature of things, normally less widely dispersed.

Many defamation cases are settled out of court. Court cases are expensive and, inevitably, involve the washing of much dirty linen in public. The usual form of settlement is a sum of money in damages and—most important for the claimant—a public retraction and apology.

If your lawyers tell you that you have a very good case, you should settle immediately.

Richard Ingrams, *journalist and editor of 'Private Eye'*

Those cases that do reach court are heard in the High Court by a judge and a jury which has to determine whether the claimant's reputation has in fact been damaged and, if so, how much they should receive in damages. The claimant has to prove that the statement in question: was indeed defamatory; did refer to the claimant; and was published by the defendant. The defendant can defend the case by disproving any of these points or can use one of the following defences:

- **Justification**
  This means that the statement was true.

- **Fair comment**
  The statement was an honest statement of opinion (rather than fact) and was in the public interest.

- **Absolute privilege**
  Statements made in court or in Parliament are protected.

- **Qualified privilege**
  These are statements made out of a legal or moral duty. For example a senior manager in a company might report to one of its directors some action(s) of the Chief Executive they believe to be damaging to the company. If the report is made in good faith, the Chief Executive cannot complain that it is defamatory, since the manager has a duty to report the facts and the director to receive them.

Demonstrations and protests

Militant demonstrations require policemen as an essential part of their ritual, to be sworn at, mocked and hated and convenient substitutes for the government.

Ben Whitaker, *lawyer, politician, and writer*

The Human Rights Act not only protects freedom of expression, it also says that citizens have the right to peaceful assembly and association—which means that they have the right to take part in demonstrations and protests. This is, however, only a qualified right, which can be restricted by the government, provided that it can show that such restrictions are 'necessary in democratic society'.

Restrictions

Some of the legal restrictions to the right to demonstrate are contained in the Public Order Act 1986, which makes it an offence to act in such a way as to make a reasonable person fear for their own safety. It defines three offences:

- **affray**, caused by an individual acting on their own;
- **violent disorder**, committed by at least three people together;
- **riot**, committed by at least twelve people together.

There are a number of other offences with which demonstrators can be charged:

- breach of the peace
- obstructing the highway
- obstructing the police
- assault.

Part B: Reference section
Contents

Glossary

abatement of a nuisance If you are suffering from a *private nuisance* you have limited rights to take action yourself to abate the nuisance. For example if your neighbour's tree overhangs your garden you can cut off the part that overhangs. In general the law isn't very keen on this type of action and you would be expected (a) to have discussed it with your neighbours first and (b) to return any of their property removed in this way (i.e. the branch of the tree).

See chapter 9 page 95

absolute privilege A defence in a case of *defamation*: statements made in court or in Parliament are protected from legal actions.

absolute discharge In a criminal case if the defendant pleads guilty or is found guilty, they are liable to be punished. Despite this the court may decide that it does not wish to impose any penalty at all. In such a case it gives the offender an absolute discharge: the crime goes on the defendant's record, but there is no punishment at all. This is a rare occurrence; a court is more likely to impose a *conditional discharge*.

ACAS The *Advisory, Conciliation, and Arbitration Service.*

See chapter 2 pages 17–20

acceptance The second essential component of a *contract*, the others being *offer*, *consideration*, *intention*, and *capacity*. For a contract to exist, one party has to accept the whole of an offer made by the other. Acceptance of only part of it, or of a modified version of it, is not acceptance but a counter offer.

accused The person being tried in a criminal case.

acquittal When someone charged with a criminal offence is found not guilty they are acquitted. Nothing goes on their record and they cannot be charged with the same offence again, even if the police find new and damning evidence against them. (At the time of writing, this right is under attack from the current administration.)

Act of Parliament A bill that has passed through Parliament and received the Royal Assent.

actual bodily harm Injuring someone so as to cause them pain or discomfort. Causing actual bodily harm is a lesser offence than *grievous bodily harm.*

adjournment A break called in a court case, either with a specific date for its resumption or *sine die* (without a date being set).

adjudication The judgment of a court or tribunal.

administration order This is an order made by a court when a company is in serious financial difficulty. An administrator is appointed to run the company in place of the board of directors and has full power over all aspects of the company's operations. While the administration order is in effect, those who are owed money by the company cannot recover goods supplied or get at the assets of the company. The administrator's aim is to rescue those parts of the company that can be rescued and if the company has to be wound up, to ensure that its assets are as valuable as possible. Creditors will then be able to recover as much of the money owed to them as possible. The court can be asked to make an administration order by the board of directors, by the members of the company, or by its creditors.

Advisory, Conciliation, and Arbitration Service (ACAS) An independent body which advises on a broad range of industrial relations issues. It publishes codes of practice on a number of matters such as disciplinary and grievance procedures. If a case goes to an *Employment Tribunal*, ACAS are informed and will offer to mediate in an attempt to avoid a full hearing.

advocate Someone who has rights of audience and is therefore qualified to plead a case in court.

affidavit A written document made under *oath* and witnessed by an authorized person. Affidavits can be used as statements of evidence in various legal proceedings.

affirm If you are a witness in a court case (or before you swear an *affidavit*) you will be asked to take the *oath.* If you object to using religious language, you can opt instead to affirm that the evidence you are going to give is true. If after making the affirmation you are found to have lied, you are guilty of *perjury*.

affirm a contract If a contract is *voidable* and you are the innocent party you may choose to withdraw from it (without penalty) or to continue with it, in which case you are said to affirm it.

See chapter 9 page 96

affray An offence under the Public Order Act 1986. 'A person is guilty of affray if he uses or threatens unlawful violence towards another and his conduct is such as would cause a person of reasonable firmness present at the scene to fear for his personal safety.' Affray is caused by one or two people acting independently. Where more are involved then the offence is either *violent disorder* or *riot*.

aggravated vehicle taking Legal term for joy-riding.

See chapter 2 pages 17–20

agreement One of the ways in which a *contract* can come to an end. The people involved may not complete the contract in every detail. Instead they may do all the things that they think are important and *agree* that the contract has been fulfilled.

aiding and abetting If a person is found guilty of a crime, other people who helped or encouraged them may also be found guilty of aiding and abetting them, even if they did not actually commit the crime themselves. 'Aiding' means giving practical help before or during the crime, for example by providing tools to a burglar or by keeping watch during the robbery. 'Abetting' means providing encouragement actually at the scene of the crime. If someone is to be found guilty of aiding and abetting, they have to have known that a crime was being committed and that their actions were contributing to it.

alibi Someone accused of a crime may say that at the time of the crime they were somewhere else. If they can prove that this was so, then it forms an effective defence. If the case is being heard in a Crown Court, then the defence team must inform the prosecution that it intends to use an alibi and give details. (In other words they can't spring it on the prosecution during the trial.)

appeal After a case has been heard in court or in a *tribunal*, one of those involved may decide that it has not been conducted fairly. If so they may decide to appeal to a higher court to have the case retried. If the appeal is allowed, then it is heard in a higher court than the original case. So, for example, a case that was originally heard in a Magistrates' Court, will be heard on appeal in a Crown Court. Crown Court cases go to the Court of Appeal; and Court of Appeal cases go to the House of Lords. There is a parallel route for civil cases.

appellant Person making an *appeal*.

appropriate adult If a young person under the age of seventeen is taken to a police station to be questioned, this must be done in the presence of an appropriate adult. This will often be a parent, but it may be a person from the local authority social services department, or some other adult.

arbitration Taking a dispute to court is slow and expensive. So disputes are often settled by arbitration. Both sides agree on an independent arbitrator and agree to be bound by the arbitrator's decision. The hearing is either in person and in private or 'on paper', where the two sides submit all their arguments in writing. Arbitration can be agreed between the two sides privately (for example as one of the terms of a *contract*), or it can be imposed by a court. The only *appeal* against an arbitrator's award is on a matter of law—the way in which the arbitrator has interpreted the meaning of the law. You can't appeal on the grounds of fairness.

arraignment When someone is accused of a crime they are taken into court and asked whether they plead guilty or not guilty to each of the crimes they are charged with. This is called the arraignment.

arrest Taking someone into custody when they are suspected of having committed an offence. The police can arrest someone if they believe they have committed (or are about to commit) an *arrestable offence*, or if they have obtained a *warrant of arrest* from a *magistrate*. Under certain circumstances, any citizen can make an arrest (see *citizen's arrest*).

arrest warrant See *warrant of arrest*.

See chapter 9 page 90

arrestable offence Traditionally the police applied to a magistrate for a warrant before making an arrest. Although this is still possible, they now have wide powers of arrest without the need for a warrant. If they find a person committing an arrestable offence, or believe that they have done so, they can arrest them. Arrestable offences are those which:

- carry a fixed sentence (e.g. murder); or
- carry a maximum sentence of five years' imprisonment or more; or
- have been made arrestable offences by Parliament.

arson Damaging or destroying property by setting fire to it. It is a form of criminal damage—if it can be proved that the person committing the act intended the damage or was *reckless* in the actions that led to the fire.

assault Behaving in such a way that the person whom you assault is reasonably afraid that you are going to do violence to them. Examples would be raising your fist to strike them, throwing something at them, or threatening them with a gun. Assault is a criminal offence and does not require any physical contact, although it cannot be purely verbal. If there is contact, then the offence becomes *battery*. In the nature of things, assault and battery often occur together.

assured shorthold tenancy A tenancy for a limited and defined period of time during which the tenant is assured of possession, provided the terms of the tenancy are fulfilled. At the end of the period of tenancy the landlord can require the tenant to leave.

See chapter 5 page 58

attachment of earnings (order) If you owe someone money or have been ordered to pay maintenance a court may order that you pay so much per week or month. They may then order your employer to deduct this sum from your wages or salary and pay it instead to the court.

Attorney General A government minister who advises the government on legal matters. Responsible for the Crown Prosecution Service, the Serious Fraud Office, and the *Director of Public Prosecutions*.

bail When someone is arrested on suspicion of having committed a criminal offence, they may be imprisoned to await trial (*remanded in custody*), or they may be released (remanded on *bail*). If so, they will be asked to promise to return to the police station when required. They also have to pay a sum of money as a guarantee that they will in fact do so. The court may require one or more people to act as sureties that the accused will appear when required. Other conditions may also be made. For example the accused may have to stay within the immediate vicinity of their home, to live in a bail hostel, or to report to the police station every day. If someone applies for bail and the prosecution object, it is up to them to demonstrate to the court why it should not be granted. For example they may argue that the defendant is likely to interfere with witnesses or to run away.

balance of probabilities This is one of the key differences between criminal and civil cases. In a criminal case the accused has to be proved guilty beyond reasonable doubt. Civil cases demand a lower level of proof: on the balance of probabilities.

Bar Council More fully, the General Council of the Bar of England and Wales. This is the body that regulates *barristers* and investigates complaints against them. It acts for barristers as the *Law Society* does for *solicitors*.

See chapter 3 page 30

barrister A lawyer who has qualified and gained the right to present a case in any court. Barristers have to be members of one of the Inns of Court and to operate as self-employed sole traders (i.e. they cannot form partnerships). Barristers work as advocates, pleading a case, but are also asked to provide opinions—detailed advice on the legal aspects of a situation (and of what might happen if it went to court). Members of the public cannot approach a barrister directly, but have to go through a solicitor. After ten years' experience, a barrister can apply to the Lord Chancellor's department to become *Queen's Counsel*, or QC. If successful they are known as 'silks', because of the gowns they wear, and are likely to be offered bigger cases.

battery Causing criminal violence to someone, for example by hitting or stabbing them or by throwing something at them. (See also *assault*.)

bench warrant A warrant to arrest someone who has been required to attend court and has failed to do so.

beneficiary Someone who inherits something from a *will*.

beyond reasonable doubt In a criminal trial the prosecution has to prove that the person accused was guilty beyond reasonable doubt. This is a higher standard of proof than that required in civil trials: see *balance of probabilities*.

bequeath To leave someone something in a *will*.

bequest Property, goods or money left to a *beneficiary* in a *will*.

Bill The wording of a law while it is passing through Parliament. It does not become the law of the land until it has received the Royal Assent. At this point it becomes an Act.

bind over A court may require someone to guarantee that they will behave in a certain way. For example, if two people are constantly rowing and one has been charged with assaulting the other, the court may bind both of them over to keep the peace for a period of a year. Both have to pay a sum of money into the court. If they break the order by fighting again, then the money is retained as a fine.

blackmail Demanding money, or other things, by threatening someone. This can include threatening to tell someone else something about the person you are threatening, or telling them that unless they do what you say you will harm them in some other way.

bona fide Latin for 'in good faith'. It is often used instead of 'genuine'.

breach of contract If you enter into a legal agreement with someone but fail to complete your side of the *contract* you are in breach of contract. In this case, the other party doesn't have to fulfil their side of the contract , and may sue you for *damages.*

See chapter 2 page 20

breach of the peace If you harm, or threaten to harm someone or their property (while they are present), you are committing a breach of the peace. If you are found guilty of a breach of the peace, the court may *bind you over* to keep the peace for a given period.

brief Written instructions to an *advocate* to plead a case on behalf of a client. In popular speech the word is also used to refer to the advocate ('I want to talk to my brief').

burden of proof In a criminal trial the prosecution has to prove the defendant guilty: the accused is assumed to be innocent until guilt is proved. Similarly in a civil case it is the *claimant* who has to prove their case. In each case, this is the burden of proof.

burglary Entering a building with the intention of committing *theft,* inflicting *grievous bodily harm*, *criminal damage*, or rape. These four are all 'burglary with intent'. If you enter a building without this intent but then steal something or inflict grievous bodily harm (or try to), you are guilty of 'burglary without intent'. If you enter the building with a weapon, then it is aggravated burglary.

by-law/bye-law A regulation made by a local authority or public authority covering the area for which it is responsible. So for example a district council makes by-laws for its district, covering such matters as dropping litter and dogs fouling pavements, while the British Airports Authority makes by-laws covering the use of its airports. The right to make by-laws is 'delegated' by Parliament to the relevant authority.

See chapter 2 page 19

capacity
(1) contract law: For a contract to be legally binding those who make it must have capacity. This means that they must be able to understand what they are agreeing to. The law assumes that people over eighteen automatically have capacity unless they were mentally incapable or drunk when the agreement was made, that the other party realized this, and the goods or services that they received were not necessaries (things necessary for their normal life). So even if a common-sense view might be that a person making an agreement was not capable of understanding what they were doing, the law may well say that they were.

See chapter 7 page 73

(2) employment law: One of the grounds on which an employee may be dismissed is if they show that they lack capacity; in other words they are unable to carry out the duties for which they were employed, for example because of chronic sickness.

care See *duty of care.*

See chapter 4 page 41

care order If a local authority believes that a child is suffering serious harm because his/her parents aren't looking after him/her properly—or that this is likely to happen—then it can apply for an order from the court to have the child put into its care. The *parental responsibility* for the child is thus transferred to the local authority.

careless driving See *driving without due care and attention.*

case law The type of law that has been developed over the centuries by the accumulation of decisions by judges and courts. It is contrasted with *statute law* which is law enacted by Parliament.

causation An important legal concept. In criminal law it is necessary for the prosecution to prove that the crime was a result of an action by the defendant: there has to be a 'chain of causation'. The defendant's action may not have been the only cause, but it must have made an important contribution to causing the result. So, for example, X has stabbed Y, who is bleeding to death. If Y can be got to the hospital in time Y's life may be saved. On the way to the hospital the ambulance is struck by the car of Z, who is drunk. As a result Y does not get to hospital in time and dies. Both X and Z have contributed to his death, but only X can be said to have caused it.

causing death by dangerous driving If someone is killed as a result of another person's *dangerous driving*, then that person is guilty of the more serious offence of causing death by dangerous driving.

See chapter 6 page 67

caution (1) When the police arrest someone, they have to tell them why (the offence which they are suspected of committing) and they have to caution them: *You do not have to say anything. But it may harm your defence if you do not mention when questioned something which you later rely on in court. Anything you do say may be given in evidence.*
(2) If the police decide not to prosecute someone who has committed an offence they may release them with a caution, a warning that if they offend again the previous offence may also be brought up again.

See chapter 9 page 91

caveat emptor Latin for 'let the buyer beware'. If you buy something from a shop or company that is in the business of selling goods to consumers you are protected by consumer law and can take action if the goods are not of satisfactory quality. But if you buy from an individual, or from a company that is not in the business of buying and selling to consumers, then you have to 'beware' and satisfy yourself that the goods are what you think they are and that they are fit for your purpose.

See chapter 8 page 83

chain of causation See *causation*.

chambers The rooms occupied by a judge while a trial is in progress. The judge may deal with some aspects of the case by talking to prosecution and defence 'in chambers'.

See chapter 3 page 29

Chancery Division of the High Court The part of the *High Court of Justice* that deals with *wills*, the ownership of real estate, *trusts*, companies, and *intellectual property*.

child safety order In recent years there has been considerable concern about bad behaviour by young children which, if left unchecked, could well lead to more serious and criminal behaviour. If a court considers that a child under ten is behaving in ways which harm other people outside the family or are socially disruptive it can impose a child safety order. The court is free to impose on the child whatever conditions it thinks appropriate, such as requiring the child to attend out-of-school activities, or to avoid meeting up with other children who are a bad influence.

See chapter 4 page 41

Child Support Agency The body responsible for ensuring that absent (non-resident) parents pay their contribution to the maintenance of their child(ren). The CSA has the job of tracking down these parents and then ensuring that they pay what is due.

See chapter 3 pages 32–33

circuit judge A judge who hears cases in the *Crown Court* and *County Court*. *Barristers* with ten years' experience and *recorders* with two years' experience may be appointed circuit judges. *Solicitors* who have qualified to appear in the County Court or the Crown Court and have ten years' experience may also be appointed.

Citizens' Advice Bureau An organization staffed by volunteers which offers free advice on a variety of issues to members of the public. A lot of their work concerns debt and social welfare matters, and they also give some legal advice, sometimes through local solicitors who offer their services.

See chapter 9 page 90

citizen's arrest If you see someone committing an *arrestable offence*, or have reason to believe that they have done so, or are about to do so, then you may *arrest* them, even if you are not a police officer. If, however, it turns out that they were innocent, then they may sue you for *false imprisonment*.

civil case A case involving a dispute between individuals or companies. See *civil law*.

civil court A court that handles civil, as opposed to criminal, cases. The first 'port of call' for civil cases is normally the *County Court*, and above that is the *High Court*.

civil jury A jury in a civil case. Most civil cases are heard without a jury, the main exceptions being fraud and libel cases.

civil law This is sometimes called private law. It is the law relating to disputes between private individuals, by contrast with public law, which relates to relationships between the citizen and the state. The main areas of civil law are *tort*, *contract*, *company law*, and *family law*.

claimant In civil law, the person who is bringing the case to court, because they consider they have been wronged in some way and are *claim*ing some redress. In the past the term for this was 'plaintiff'.

class action This occurs when a group of people have all suffered the same wrong and take action together in the *civil court*. This is most commonly in cases of *negligence*—for example a group of workers who have all suffered ill health because of claimed negligence on the part of the employer. The case is heard as a class action to determine its validity and then each individual case is heard to determine how much each person is to receive in compensation.

clean break In divorce, the principle that the parties should agree a division of their property in such a way that no maintenance is then to be paid by either. Where there are dependent children involved this may not be possible.

codicil A document which adds to or changes a *will*. It has to be signed and witnessed in the same way as a will.

cohabitants Unmarried people living together as man and wife.

cohabitation Part of the legal definition of marriage: living together and, by implication, having sexual relations.

cohabitee See *cohabitants*.

Commission for Racial Equality (CRE) An independent body which advises and makes recommendations on racial and ethnic issues. Its brief is to promote racial equality and to pursue discrimination in the workplace and in society generally.

Commissioner for Local Administration The *ombudsman* responsible for dealing with complaints against Local Authorities.

committal proceedings If a case is *triable either way* (i.e. in the Magistrates' Court or the Crown Court), the magistrates may decide it should be tried in the Crown Court, or the defendant may opt to be tried in the Crown Court. In these cases the magistrates have the responsibility of hearing and assessing the evidence for the prosecution and then committing the case to the Crown Court. Alternatively if the defence agrees, the prosecution may submit its evidence in written form, in which case there is no hearing.

See chapter 5 page 51

commonhold A proposed form of land holding whereby leaseholders of flats would be able jointly to buy the leasehold of the land on which the flats stand.

common law Law that has developed from the decisions of judges, also called *case law*.

Community Legal Service fund (CLS fund) The system replacing legal aid, by which people who qualify can receive assistance with their legal expenses in civil and family cases.

community rehabilitation order (Formerly 'probation order'.) An alternative sentence to imprisonment. The offender agrees to spend a period of time (six months to three years) under the supervision of a probation officer. The offender has to report to the probation officer at set intervals and there may be other conditions imposed.

community sentence A group of alternatives to imprisonment, commonly *community rehabilitation* (probation), or *community service*.

community service order A court sentence that is an alternative to prison. The offender is sentenced to do a number of hours' work of value to the community, such as working on a conservation project. The work is supervised by a probation officer.

company law A branch of *civil law* relating to companies. It covers such topics as the filing of proper accounts and the responsibilities of directors.

compensation order In some criminal cases the court orders the convicted defendant to pay compensation to the victim of the crime.

compensatory award An employee who has been dismissed unfairly can take their case to an *Employment Tribunal*. If the Tribunal finds that the dismissal was unfair it can order the employer to take the employee back. If this is not practicable or reasonable, then the employee will be awarded compensation. The size of the basic award will depend on the employee's age, length of service, and salary, but the Tribunal may also make a compensatory award, to compensate the employee for loss of prospects, future salary, and so on.

See chapter 7 page 77

compos mentis Latin for 'of sound mind'.

concurrent sentence When a defendant is convicted of two separate offences and sentenced to imprisonment, the prison sentences can run at the same time (concurrently) or one after the other (consecutively).

conditional discharge Sometimes a criminal court does not consider that an offender should be punished in any way even when they have pleaded guilty or been found guilty (for example if the offence is very minor). In such a situation although the crime still goes down on the offender's record, the court may discharge the prisoner on condition that they do not re-offend in a given period (up to three years). If the offender does re-offend within that period, they can be brought back to court and punished for the original offence.

See chapter 7 page 73

conduct In employment law one of the grounds on which an employer can dismiss an employee is because of their behaviour, or conduct. See also *gross misconduct* and *ordinary misconduct*.

consecutive sentence See *concurrent sentence*.

See chapter 2 page 18

consideration One of the requirements for a legal contract to exist is that there should be some benefit to both parties who are entering into the agreement. There has to be an exchange of money, goods, or services. This is known as the 'consideration'. If only one side offers money, goods, or services but gets nothing in return, then legally it is not a contract but a 'bare promise'.

consortium Latin for *cohabitation*.

conspiracy An agreement between two or more people to commit a criminal offence. They do not then have to go on to commit the crime, or even to attempt to, for the conspiracy to have taken place. By its nature, conspiracy can be difficult to prove beyond reasonable doubt.

See chapter 7 page 77

constructive dismissal Where an employer treats a worker in such a way as to force them to resign. In such cases the worker can take their case to an *Employment Tribunal* and argue that it is *unfair dismissal*.

contact order One of the orders a court may make in a divorce case, to ensure that one of the parents has access to the child(ren).

contempt of court A number of offences are regarded as contempt of court. These include:

- a refusal to carry out the judgment of the court;
- disclosing confidential documents used in the case;
- interfering with the jury;

- violent or threatening behaviour inside the court;
- attacking the way the judge is handling the case;
- publishing material that might prejudice the chance of a trial being fair.

If a judge finds a person guilty of contempt that person can be fined or sent to prison.

contract An agreement between two parties that is legally binding on both. It has five essential components. One part has to make an *offer* which the other *accepts*. There must be some *consideration* (which involves the transfer of goods and/or services between the two parties). Both must have the *intention* to enter into a legal agreement and both must have the *capacity* (i.e. be in their right minds at the time the deal is struck). If one party then breaks the contract, by failing to fulfil their part of the agreement, the other may sue for damages for *breach of contract*.

See chapter 2 pages 17–20

contributory negligence In a civil case where a *claimant* sues the *defendant* for *damages*, the defendant may claim that the claimant contributed to his/her own loss. For example, the claimant Mr Green slips on an oily floor at his place of work and is injured. He sues his employer, Brown & Co., for *negligence*. Brown & Co. argue that Green contributed to his own downfall because at the time of the accident he was running across the shop floor, despite notices forbidding this. Although the oil should have been cleaned off the floor (Brown & Co.'s negligence), Green should not have been running (Green's contributory negligence).

conveyance When a house is sold, if it is not registered at the *Land Registry*, a document has to be drawn up transferring ownership from the seller to the buyer. This is a conveyance.

conveyancing Transferring ownership of land and/or buildings from one person to another. In the past this had to be done by a solicitor. Now it can be done by licensed conveyancers, building societies, and banks. Individuals can also do their own conveyancing.

See chapter 4 page 47

coroner Coroners were originally appointed by the Crown to work in a particular area and guard the Crown's rights over its own private property. They are still appointed by central government and work locally, but now their main role is to investigate unnatural or violent deaths. They may order an autopsy (post-mortem), an examination of the body to determine the cause of death and other relevant factors. The coroner holds an *inquest* into the cause of death.

corporate liability Corporations can be held responsible for their actions and sued or prosecuted. So they are liable for their actions just like an individual.

corporation Certain organizations, such as registered companies, local authorities, and others (e.g. the BBC) are said to have 'legal personalities'. This means that in the eyes of the law they exist independently of the people who work for them. They can make contracts and be sued or prosecuted.

corroboration Confirmation of a statement that has been made in court by the production of physical evidence or the statement of a witness.

costs *Civil cases* normally end with a judgment that one side has made its case. Both sides will have suffered considerable expense in legal fees, paying expert witnesses and court dues. The judgment usually includes a provison that the losing side should pay the costs of the winners. This doesn't always happen; sometimes the judge does not award costs because there was no need for the victor to have brought the case in the first place. Judges also sometimes only award a proportion of the costs, leaving the victors to pay the rest of their costs themselves.

See chapter 3 page 28

County Court The local courts which hear *civil cases.* A large number of cases are conducted in the County Court, including personal injuries, debt, racial and sexual discrimination, and undefended divorce cases.

See chapter 3 page 27

Court of Appeal As its name suggests, this court hears cases that have been referred to it because those involved consider that they have not received justice from a lower court. In *civil* *cases*, the Court of Appeal hears appeals from *County Courts* and and the *High Court*. In *criminal cases* it hears appeals from the *Crown Court*.

covenant A promise made between two people. Covenants often form part of a larger agreement. See *restrictive covenant*.

crime An action that the law defines as a public wrong (as opposed to actions which are private wrongs to which the individual has to seek redress in a civil court). So if A attacks B and breaks B's arm, A has committed a crime, since society considers that this kind of behaviour damages not just B, but society at large. A has also wronged B personally and may, for example, have prevented B from working. So B is entitled to sue A for damages in the civil court.

See chapter 2 pages 12–13

criminal case A case in which the defendant is charged with having committed a *crime*. Most prosecutions in criminal cases are brought by the Crown (via the *Crown Prosecution Service*).

criminal damage If a person deliberately damages property belonging to someone else, or if they cause damage by behaving *recklessly*, they are guilty of criminal damage and, if found guilty, can be punished by up to ten years in prison.

Crown Court A court in which *criminal cases* are heard by a judge. The verdict is the responsibility of a *jury*.

See chapter 3 page 26

Crown Prosecution Service (CPS) The organization responsible for organizing the prosecution in criminal cases. Its head is the *Director of Public Prosecutions*. The CPS is independent of the police, whose job is to assemble evidence and then present the case to them for consideration.

See chapter 3 page 34

curfew order An order made by a court as a way of controlling the movements of someone over sixteen found guilty of criminal act(s). For example the offender might be required to stay inside their own house between 6p.m. and 6a.m.

custodial sentence Imprisonment.

damages In a *civil case* when the *claimant* is successful the *defendant* pays a sum of money as compensation for the wrong they have suffered. These are the damages. In a case for *breach of contract*, the damages are defined by the actual financial loss suffered by the injured party.

See chapter 6 page 67

dangerous driving It is difficult to pin down when careless driving shades into dangerous driving, but the more serious offence is characterized by a deliberate disregard for other road users and behaviour which is likely to cause (or has caused) danger to others. Drivers charged with dangerous driving are usually charged with careless driving as well—as a kind of insurance policy for police and prosecution. A person found guilty of dangerous driving can be sent to prison as well as losing their licence.

debtor-creditor agreement If you borrow money from a bank or other institution and there are no restrictions on how the money is to be spent, then you have a debtor-creditor agreement with the bank. Some personal loans are examples of this, as are withdrawals from a cash machine using a credit card. Such agreements are regulated by the Consumer Credit Act 1974.

debtor-creditor-supplier agreement An agreement by which you borrow money for a specific purchase, and there is a link between the supplier and the lender. For example if you buy a car on hire purchase you are borrowing the money for the purchase either from the manufacturer or from a finance house tied in to the manufacturer. If you buy goods in a shop using a credit card there is an agreement between the retailer and the bank that the credit transaction will be honoured. In each case you can only spend the money you have borrowed on a specific item. Such agreements are regulated by the Consumer Credit Act 1974.

deceit In the law of *tort*, if you deceive someone and on the basis of that false information they then act in such a way as to suffer some kind of damage, they can bring a case of deceit against you. For example, someone selling a second-hand car who says that it once belonged to a famous racing driver (which would enhance its resale value) when this is untrue, is guilty of deceit.

decree absolute The final stage in a divorce case, and the moment at which the divorce is complete and the former partners can legally marry again. It is in the form of an order from the court.

decree nisi The last but one stage in a divorce case. The Latin word 'nisi' means 'unless'. A decree nisi states that the divorce will be completed unless any objections are made. Six weeks later a *decree absolute* can be applied for.

deed A legal document in which you commit yourself to something. Once you have signed it you cannot change your mind. A deed has to be in writing, signed, dated, and witnessed.

de facto Latin for 'in fact'. In law it is contrasted with de jure ('in/by law').

defendant In a criminal trial the person being tried for a crime; in a civil trial the person being sued by the *claimant*.

defamation If A makes public a statement that damages B's reputation, B may sue A for defamation. A has harmed B personally (which is a *tort*) and B may require recompense in the form of damages; B will also want the truth made public. See also *slander* and *libel.*

See chapter 9 page 94

delegated legislation Parliament is the source of all law, but it does not necessarily make all laws itself. Sometimes it passes down (delegates) its law-making powers to others. It delegates to local authorities the power to make *by-laws* covering certain activities within their own area. It can also pass 'enabling legislation' which delegates to government ministers the power to make *statutory instruments*—in effect, to make laws. This is often unpopular with parliamentarians and others because statutory instruments aren't debated in Parliament and are seen as undemocratic.

descendants A person's children, their children, and so on—a term used in *wills*.

desertion If a husband leaves his wife against her wishes, or vice versa, and ceases to live in the marital home, it is desertion. Desertion for a period of two years is a ground for divorce, because it is evidence that the marriage has irretrievably broken down.

diminished responsibility A defence against murder. The defendant claims that at the time of the crime they were in a mental state short of insanity but such as to prevent them being able to make 'normal' judgments of the results or implications of their actions. This state of mental imbalance might be caused by a physical condition (e.g. medication or injury), or a psychological condition such as depression.

directive In European Union law, the Commission issues directives, which member states are required to put into effect. They have a certain flexibility in this, but are required to enforce the objectives of the directive through national law. In England this is done though *statutory instruments*.

See chapter 3 page 34

Director of Public Prosecutions The head of the *Crown Prosecution Service* responsible to the *Attorney General*.

See chapter 2 page 20

discharge of contract When a contract comes to an end. This can happen in a number of ways: the parties involved can each fulfil their side of the contract; they can agree to do something else, thus making a new contract which replaces the old (*agreement*); it may become impossible for the contract to be fulfilled (e.g. through the death of one of the parties); or one party may fail to fulfil their side of the contract (*breach of contract*).

disclaimer A term with two meanings in law: **(1)** giving up a right or property for some reason, but usually because it is not to your advantage. For example your uncle may leave you £10,000 and full ownership of a company which is losing £20,000 a week. You can take the money but disclaim the company.
(2) In the law of tort you can make a disclaimer and provided

people know this they cannot sue you for negligence. For example, the following disclaimer is to be found in a book published by *Rough Guides*: 'The publishers and authors have done their best to ensure the accuracy and currency of all information in *The Rough Guide to Andalucia*, however they can accept no responsibility for any loss, injury or inconvenience sustained by any traveller as a result of information or advice contained in the guide.'

disclosure of evidence The obligation of each side in a civil or criminal trial to inform the other side about certain aspects of their case. In a criminal case the prosecution has to inform the defence of anything which seriously weakens the prosecution case. The defence has to tell the prosecution roughly what the defence case will be and if it intends to use an *alibi* what the alibi is. In civil cases both sides have to disclose documents that they are using as part of their case and other documents they know about which may affect the case either way.

discrimination In employment law and in certain other areas of life, it is illegal to discriminate against a person on grounds of sex, race, or disability.

See chapter 9 pages 92-93

disqualification from driving One of the penalties for certain motoring offences is to have your driving licence taken away for a period of time. This can happen in three ways: if you build up twelve penalty points in a three-year period; if you commit an offence for which disqualification is automatic (e.g. drink driving); if you commit an offence for which the court has the power to disqualify and feels that in your case it is the most suitable sentence (e.g. driving while uninsured).

district judge A judge who hears small civil cases in the County Court (typically small claims and family law cases). District judges are appointed from the ranks of solicitors and barristers with at least seven years' experience.

See chapter 3 pages 32-33

district judge (Magistrates' Court) In large centres of population it is not feasible to have all the work of the

Magistrates' Court done by part-time *Justices of the Peace*, so paid district judges, working full-time, are employed. They have the same powers as two JPs and are appointed from the ranks of solicitors and barristers with at least seven years' experience.

domestic violence Violence that takes place in the home of a married or unmarried couple. It can be punished under the criminal law, but increasingly the law is used to remove the causes. Under the Family Law Act 1996 a court can order the guilty party to stop (a 'non-molestation order') or to leave the home (an 'occupation order').

driving without due care and attention The full definition of careless driving is 'driving without due care and attention, or without reasonable consideration for other persons using the road.' If convicted the driver has his/her licence endorsed and may be punished by disqualification from driving, and a fine of up to £2,500 (although something in the region of £200 is more common).

duress Forcing someone to do something against their will by threats. In criminal cases duress can be a defence against most crimes except murder and treason. Defendants using this defence have to prove that they or some member of their immediate family was threatened with death or serious injury and that they believed the threat to be a real one. (And that a reasonable person would have behaved in the same way.) In civil law a contract is *void* if one of the parties was forced into it by physical or financial duress.

duty of care Each individual has a duty to make sure that by their careless behaviour other people aren't hurt. For example, if A is walking down the street carrying a ladder and swings round carelessly thus knocking B to the ground and injuring B, A has 'breached' (broken) his/her duty of care and B can sue A for *negligence*.

See chapter 5 page 52

easement If someone other than the owner of a property has some rights over their land, it is called an easement. For example A's drains may run across B's front garden, or A may have the right to cross B's garden to get to theirs. Each of these rights is an easement. As owner, B must not do anything to interfere with those rights; B may not, for example, dig up the drains, or block off the right of way with a fence.

Employment Tribunal A *tribunal* which hears cases relating to employment, such as charges of *discrimination* and *unfair dismissal*.

See chapter 7 page 77

enabling act If Parliament wishes to delegate the right to make laws, it can pass an enabling act which allows another body such as a local authority or a government department to issue regulations. This is how local authorities are enabled to issue *by-laws* and Ministers to issue *statutory instruments*. See also *delegated legislation*.

Equal Opportunities Commission The independent body set up by law to promote and monitor equal opportunities for both sexes and to enable individuals to fight sex discrimination.

See Resources page 153

equitable According to *equity* or natural justice.

equity A word with a number of meanings. In its broader sense, it refers to natural justice; the principles of the law (as opposed to the letter). In a narrower sense it refers to situations where in the past there were found to be gaps in English civil law, cases which could not be sorted out by referring to previous court rulings. Such instances can be referred to the High Court, which will decide such cases on principles of equity.

estate The property belonging to a person less anything they may owe. It is divided into *real property* and *personal property*. At the time of a person's death the value of their estate is assessed for taxation and then distributed in accordance with their *will*.

European Convention on Human Rights A document that was compiled after the Second World War setting out the basic human rights, which were guaranteed by the signatories. Although Britain signed it in 1969, it was not incorporated into law until 1996. Breaches of the convention are now handled in British courts, although individuals can also appeal direct to the *European Court of Human Rights*.

See chapter 9 page 88

European Court of Human Rights A court established under the European Convention on Human Rights to hear cases alleging breaches of the convention. It sits in Strasbourg and although its judgments are not binding on member states they are usually obeyed.

See chapter 9 page 88

European Court of Justice The court of the European Community which hears cases relating to E.U. law.

See chapter 3 page 24

exclusion clause In a contract, a clause which excludes liability if something specified happens. For example, when you pay to use a car park, you are entering into a contract with the owner. If your car is damaged while parked there, you might decide to sue the owner for not looking after your car while it was there. This is why most car parks have a notice stating that the owner accepts no liability for any loss or damage caused to cars parked. An exclusion clause must be clear and either well established (like the car park notice) or specifically drawn to the attention of the other party (as in a written contract).

exclusion order An order made by a court which forbids someone convicted of an offence from going to a particular place. For example someone with a record of drunken behaviour who has been convicted of assault in a particular public house could be excluded from going there for a stated period of time.

Executive That part of the constitution with responsibility for administering the laws. In England, this is Her Majesty's Government.

See chapter 3 page 21

executor One or more people given the task of carrying out the wishes expressed in a will. They may be members of the family or personal friends, or possibly a bank or solicitor. When the *testator* dies the executors are responsible for organizing the funeral arrangements and carrying out the provisions of the will.

See chapter 4 page 49

exemplary damages When damages are awarded in a case of tort, the court may wish to punish the offender by awarding the claimant damages that are greater than the amount that would normally be awarded (to compensate them for financial loss suffered). For example a drugs company might continue to sell a product that was harmful after it had discovered the dangers of the product. The company might be prepared to risk being sued for negligence because it reckoned that the profits to be made outweighed the damages it was likely to have to pay. The court could take this into account when assessing damages and set them high enough to punish the company and deter others from behaving in this way in the future.

express term Part of a contract that is 'spelled out' or made explicit in the wording—as opposed to an *implied term*.

See chapter 2 page 19

fair comment A defence against a case of *defamation*. The defendant using this defence has to prove that the statement made was an expression of opinion rather than fact, that it was made without any wish to hurt the claimant, and that the defendant believed it to be true.

See chapter 9 pages 94–95

false imprisonment A form of *trespass to person*. If you remove or impede someone's freedom of movement you are falsely imprisoning them, for example by shutting them up in a room or by tying them up so that they cannot escape. This is a *tort* and the victim can sue the guilty person for *damages*.

Family Division of the High Court The part of the *High Court* that deals with family cases and some probate cases.

See chapter 3 page 29

Family Panel (in Magistrates' Court) Family cases such as those concerning maintenance and the welfare of children are handled in Magistrates' Courts by specially trained magistrates forming a Family Panel.

fast track cases In civil law cases which involve sums of more than the *small claims* limit (£5,000) but less than £15,000 can be made 'fast track'. The various stages are subject to a strict timetable usually leading to a final hearing within thirty weeks. As well as ensuring a swifter decision, the fast track process is intended to limit the costs of those involved.

fiduciary A word used to describe a relationship involving trust and confidence, with the related responsibilities that this brings.

fiduciary duties of directors The relationship between directors of a company and the shareholders is regarded as a *fiduciary* one. They have a fiduciary duty to the company, which means that they must work for the benefit of the company and therefore avoid any conflict of interest (for example in situations where they are directors of two companies that are in competition with each other).

fiduciary relationship Common *fiduciary* relationships are those between a solicitor and client, and a trustee and those who benefit from the *trust*.

fit for purpose The Sale of Goods Act 1979 uses this term to define the required standard for goods that are offered for sale. It means that a particular item should be suitable for the purposes for which most people would normally expect to use it. If a customer has asked for an item for a particular purpose and the retailer sells them a product, then it is expected to be suitable for the specific purpose described.

fraud Using false statements or other forms of misrepresentation to gain an advantage to yourself; for example, lying to cheat someone out of their money. If you behave in a fraudulent way in a contract, it makes the contract *voidable* on the grounds of misrepresentation.

See chapter 9 pages 88–89

freedom of association One of the rights guaranteed in the European Convention on Human Rights (and brought into UK law by the Human Rights Act 1998): 'Everyone has the right to freedom of peaceful assembly and to freedom of association with others, including the right to form and join trade unions for the protection of his interests.' This right is, however, quite heavily qualified by a number of laws in the UK relating to public order.

freedom of the person One of the rights guaranteed in the European Convention on Human Rights (and brought into UK law by the Human Rights Act 1998): 'Everyone has the right to liberty and security of person.' There are a number of people excepted from this, including: those who have committed or are believed to have committed criminal offences, illegal immigrants, and those in the process of being deported.

See chapter 9 pages 88–89

freedom of speech One of the rights guaranteed in the European Convention on Human Rights (and brought into UK law by the Human Rights Act 1998): 'Everyone has the right of freedom of expression. This right shall include freedom to hold opinions and to receive and impart information and ideas without interference . . . ' There are a number of limitations to this, including *defamation*.

See chapter 9 pages 88–89

freehold A form of land ownership. The owner has permanent control of the land for their own enjoyment—by contrast with *leasehold* which is for a limited period.

See chapter 5 page 51

frustration In contract when a contract cannot be fulfilled because of circumstances beyond the control of the parties, for example if one of them dies.

See chapter 2 page 20

garden leave A clause used in employment contracts (especially for senior managers) which allows a company to retain an employee for the period of notice (possibly quite lengthy) so that they cannot go off and work for a rival. During this period the employee is paid and receives all the normal benefits, but they are not required (or, sometimes, even allowed) to go on working.

garnishee order A court order used when a defendant is shown to owe money to a claimant. If the defendant has bank or savings accounts, the court can require the bank or building society to pay part or all of the debt out of the account(s) to the claimant.

grant of probate A certificate granted by the Probate Registry allowing the *executors* of a *will* to distribute the proceeds of the *estate* to those named in the will. Before it can be issued, the executors or their representatives have to complete forms

See chapter 4 page 49

setting out in detail among other things: the contents of the estate, with valuations of non-monetary items; amounts owed to and by the person who has died; and tax liability.

grievous bodily harm Serious harm to a person, which may take the form of a physical injury or psychiatric harm (or a combination of the two). Causing grievous bodily harm is a more serious offence than causing *actual bodily harm*.

See chapter 7 page 74

gross misconduct Misconduct serious enough for an employee to be sacked out of hand. It includes, for example, theft, violence, and sexual harassment.

gross negligence See *negligence*.

habeas corpus Latin for 'you shall have the body'. If someone has been imprisoned and wishes to question the legality of this, they can apply to the High Court for a writ of habeas corpus. The imprisoned person then has to be brought to court for the question to be decided. It is a fundamental right of the individual under English law, because it is designed to guarantee that citizens can only be detained in accordance with the law and not in an arbitrary way.

See chapter 3 page 29

High Court of Justice The main court for *civil cases*. It has three divisions: *Chancery Division, Family Division,* and *Queen's Bench Division*.

High Court Judge A judge who hears *civil cases* in the High Court, or more serious cases (such as murder) in the *Crown Court*. High Court Judges are usually appointed from the ranks of experienced *Queen's Counsels*, but *circuit judges* may also be promoted to the High Court.

See chapter 3 page 21

House of Lords The upper house of Parliament. At the time of writing it is in a process of transition (or so we are told). Its chief function is in scrutinizing (examining in detail, criticizing, and amending) *bills* passed to it from the House of Commons. After this process the bill is returned to the Commons, which can accept or reject the Lords' proposals. Eventually the House Of Commons has the last say, but bills may be lost if time runs out. This gives the Lords, who include many talented lawyers and lay people, a certain power. The House of Lords is also the highest and final court of appeal in England for both civil and criminal cases, although by tradition this function is only carried out by the eleven Law Lords under the *Lord Chancellor*.

See note on page 27

Human Rights Act 1998 The statute which brought the *European Convention on Human Rights* fully into UK law. Before it was passed, all cases had to be taken to the *European Court of Human Rights*.

See chapter 9 pages 88–89

implied term A term that is not stated in a contract (as *express terms* are) but is nevertheless part of it because of legislation covering the subject matter of the contract (for example the various statutes that govern employment are implied terms of a contract of employment), or because of custom.

See chapter 2 page 19

in camera When the press and public are excluded from a case, it is 'in camera'. This is done in cases involving children and also those that concern national security. See *in curia.*

incitement persuading another person to commit a criminal offence. It is an offence even if the other person does nothing at all.

in curia Latin for 'in open court'.

indemnity clause In a contract between A and B, A may agree to pay B compensation if B has to pay damages because B is in breach of a contract or is found to be negligent. For example publishing contracts require authors to indemnify the publisher if the publisher is successfully sued for libel. If an indemnity clause is considered by a court to be unreasonable it will not be upheld.

indictable offence the most serious type of criminal offence (e.g. rape, robbery with violence, murder) which must be tried in a *Crown Court*.

indictment When someone is charged with one or more criminal offences, an indictment is drawn up listing them. The defendant is then required to plead guilty or not guilty to each charge on the indictment.

infanticide In general terms this means killing a child. In English law it is the word used to describe the offence of a mother killing her own child while it is less than one year old, while she is mentally disturbed after its birth.

injunction An order by a court instructing a person to act, or not to act in a particular way. For example a neighbour who is guilty of causing a nuisance by making excessive noise at night may be ordered to stop such behaviour in the future, or a violent husband may be ordered not to attempt to go near the wife he has been abusing.

inquest A hearing by a *coroner* to investigate the cause of a violent or sudden death.

insolvency When a person or a company has insufficient funds to pay what is owed, (s)he or it is insolvent. In the case of a company, when this happens anyone who is owed money can ask the court to make an *administration order* so that the company can be wound up and its creditors paid as much as is available.

See chapter 8 page 87

intellectual property The ownership of intangible things you have created. This includes texts, music, software, business systems, and inventions. Intellectual property is protected by the law in England and, to a degree, internationally. The Copyright, Designs, and Patents Act of 1988, with subsequent amendments, is the main legislation in England and copyright is further protected by the European Union Copyright Directive which was due to pass into UK law in 2003.

See chapter 2 page 13

intention An important part of *mens rea* or guilty mind. For many crimes, for example murder, it is necessary for the prosecution to prove that the defendant *intended* to commit the criminal act.

intestacy The state of dying *intestate*.

intestate If you have not made a *will*, you die intestate, without any heirs having been named. If this happens a court will decide to whom your *estate* should be distributed.

See chapter 4 page 48

involuntary conduct Behaviour that was not done knowingly and willingly by the person concerned because of a mental or physical condition or because they are acting under *duress*. This can be a defence against a criminal charge.

JP A Justice of the Peace, or *magistrate*.

joint tenancy One of two ways in which two people can own a freehold property together. A joint tenancy means that if one joint tenant dies their rights in the property automatically pass to the other(s). See also *tenancy in common*.

judicial review A way of appealing to the *High Court* against a ruling by a lower court, a tribunal, or similar body. The judges making the judicial review consider whether the law was misinterpreted, or there was something wrong with the procedure, or the decision was completely unreasonable.

judiciary The judges, who have the responsibility for interpreting the law and resolving disputes between litigants.

jurisdiction If a court has the power to deal with a matter, it is said to be within its jurisdiction.

Justice of the Peace A *magistrate*.

justices' clerk A qualified lawyer who advises *magistrates* during a trial in a *Magistrates' Court*.

justification A defence against *defamation*: the statement complained of is shown to be true.

See chapter 9 page 94

Land Registry Most land in England and Wales is now registered. This means that details of the property, its ownership, and any charges (*mortgages, easements, restrictive covenants*) are held by one of the regional Land Registry offices.

Law Lords (Lords of Appeal in Ordinary) Eleven of the most eminent lawyers in the land are awarded peerages and sit in the *House of Lords*. When cases go to the House of Lords on appeal they represent the House of Lords.

See note on page 27

Law Officers of the Crown In England these are the *Attorney General* and the *Solicitor General*.

Law Society The body responsible for overseeing the activities of *solicitors*. It controls admission to the profession and hears complaints of professional misconduct.

lay magistrate Most *magistrates* are unpaid and have no formal legal qualification ('lay'). A few are paid and legally qualified ('stipendiary'). To be a lay magistrate you must be between the ages of twenty-one and sixty-five, live within range of the Magistrates' Court, and be prepared to serve at least twenty-six days a year.

See chapter 5 page 51

leasehold A form of landowning limited by time. By contrast with freehold, which means owning land for ever, leasehold means that you own it for a fixed period of time. During that period you have almost the same rights as a freeholder, but the person who owns the freehold retains certain rights. For example, flats are usually sold leasehold and the owner of the freehold often has the right to enter properties for the purposes of maintenance and repair.

legislation The body of law created by Parliament.

legislature The body responsible for creating statute law. In England this is the two Houses of Parliament.

liability This term has two meanings: **(1)** an amount owed to someone; **(2)** a person's legal responsibility.

libel *Defamation* that is published in some permanent form, such as a printed book, a TV programme, or an email.

See chapter 5 pages 54–55

licensed conveyancer Someone who has a licence to do the legal work of *conveyancing,* but who is not a solicitor. To become one you have to take an exam regulated by the Council for Licensed Conveyancers.

lien This term comes from an old French word meaning 'tie'. In law it is used to refer to a person's right to hold another person's goods until they have done what they are legally required to do. Many garages, for example, will not release a repaired car to the owner until the owner has paid for the repairs.

limitation of actions In civil cases you have to bring a legal action within a certain period of the breach of contract or tort. Once that period has elapsed you can no longer open proceedings for damages. The period of time varies according to the type of action to be taken.

limited company A company registered under the Companies Act whose members only have a limited liability for the company's debts. Most limited companies are owned by shareholders or are 'limited by guarantee' (these are usually not-for-profit companies). Shareholders' liability for the company's debts is only as much as the face value of the shares they own. In a company limited by guarantee, the members only guarantee to pay a nominal amount (e.g. £5) if the company has to be wound up. The name of limited companies must include either 'Limited' ('Ltd'), in the case of private companies or 'public limited company' ('plc') in the case of public companies.

limited liability See *limited company*.

litigant Someone engaged in *litigation* either on their own account or through the services of a *barrister* or *solicitor*.

litigation Taking legal action.

Lord Chancellor The head of the judiciary, the body of judges, a member of the cabinet, and the person responsible for appointing judges and QCs. He is also effectively the Speaker of the House of Lords.

See note on page 27

Lord Chief Justice The second most senior judge, after the Lord Chancellor.

loss of amenity When you sue someone in a case of tort you are often, in effect, saying that they have prevented you from

See chapter 2 pages 14–17

doing something you ought to be able to do (e.g. if it is a case of negligence and your arm has been broken, you are no longer able to use that arm in the way that you should). This loss is the loss of amenity.

magistrate Someone who hears cases in a *Magistrates' Court*. Magistrates are unpaid, but receive some training, and work on a part-time basis.

Magistrates' Court The lowest level of court in which cases are heard by *magistrates*.

See chapter 4 page 41

maintenance order An order made by a court for a parent to contribute financially towards the support of a spouse or child. Orders for the support of children are now normally handled by the *Child Support Agency*.

See chapter 2 page 13

malice aforethought A key part of the definition of *murder*; the *mens rea* for this crime. Confusingly, it does not necessarily mean that the offender felt malice towards the victim nor that the crime was planned in advance. It means that at the time the act was committed the offender either intended to kill the victim or to cause them grievous bodily harm and that death was the result.

malicious prosecution Occasionally a person is prosecuted not in the cause of justice but out of personal malice. If the prosecution fails, the person bringing the charge can themselves be charged, with malicious prosecution. An action for malicious prosecution will only succeed if the original prosecution was unsuccessful, it was brought without good reason, and its intention was malicious.

manslaughter A killing that is not a murder but which was against the law and was not accidental. There are two types of manslaughter: voluntary and involuntary. Voluntary manslaughter covers actions which would be murder, but the circumstances mean that the severity of the crime is reduced (for example *diminished responsibility*, and suicide pacts). Involuntary manslaughter covers cases where the death is caused by gross *negligence* or is the result of a criminal action that was likely to lead to danger to the victim.

matrimonial home The flat or house that a married couple use as their home. If there is a dispute, a court can make an occupation order deciding which of the couple may live in the home. This is based on need, not necessarily ownership.

Memorandum and Articles of Association The document defining the aims and ownership of a company. The Memorandum describes the company and its shareholding; the Articles contain the rules for appointment of directors and other administrative rules.

mens rea *Mens rea* is Latin for 'guilty mind'. A crime is a criminal act committed with a 'guilty mind'. The law distinguishes different degrees in this. For some crimes, like murder, it has to be proved that there was specific intent: when X raised the axe he specifically intended to kill Y. For other crimes, it is necessary to prove recklessness or negligence by the perpetrator. There is a further group of crimes in which the perpetrator's state of mind is of no importance. If you are caught by a police speed trap breaking the speed limit it makes no difference at all whether you intended to or not; the simple fact of exceeding the limit is sufficient. Crimes of this kind are referred to as absolute or strict liability offences.

See chapter 2 page 13

merchantable quality The older term for *satisfactory quality*.

minor A person under the age of eighteen. (The law sets a variety of age limits for minors—see page 42.)

miscarriage of justice Occasions when someone is wrongly convicted of a crime they did not commit. Possible miscarriages of justice are investigated by the Criminal Cases Review Commission.

misrepresentation In a contract, 'misrepresentation' means stating something as true when it is not. If misrepresentation is proved, then the contract is not binding. Misrepresentation may be innocent (an honest mistake), negligent (a mistake that the person should have taken care to avoid), or fraudulent (deliberate). A person who is guilty of negligent or fraudulent misrepresentation can be sued for damages.

mitigation (1) When a person has been convicted of a *crime*, the defence may make a plea of mitigation, urging the judge that because of the offender's circumstances the penalty should not be too severe.
(2) In *contract* law, when a contract is *breached* the innocent party is expected to do as much as possible to reduce the loss to themselves. This is known as mitigation of loss.

M'Naghten Rules The rules defining when insanity can be used as a defence in a criminal case. The burden is on the defence to prove insanity. It has to show that the defendant either did not know what they were doing or knew what they were doing but did not know that it was wrong.

See chapter 5 page 57

mortgage In everyday language we use the word 'mortgage' to mean a loan we get from a bank or building society to buy a house. Legally what happens is that we get a loan and in return grant a mortgage to the lender, giving them rights over the property. These include the right to take possession of the property, whether or not you have failed to make the promised repayments. If you do fail to keep up with payments they can take possession of the property and sell it to recover the money they have lent. In addition your right to do what you like with the property may be restricted. For example if you wish to let the property you may have to ask the lender's permission.

mortgagee The person or institution who lends money and is granted a *mortgage* on a property.

mortgagor The person who borrows money and grants a *mortgage* to the lender.

multi-track case In *civil law* a more complex, large-scale case, one which cannot be handled by the *fast track* procedure. Multi-track cases take longer and are more expensive.

murder homicide (killing someone) with *malice aforethought*. A more serious crime than *manslaughter*.

natural justice the rules of fairness which are supposed to govern all legal decisions: that justice should be even-handed; that both sides of the case should have a fair hearing; and that no one should be a judge in their own case.

negligence a type of *tort* caused by failure in the *duty of care*. If you hurt someone or damage their property because you haven't taken sufficient care, then they may sue you for damages (repairs to their goods or compensation for their injuries). If the failure in the duty of care was very great, then the offence is referred to as gross negligence. If a person is killed as a result of gross negligence, the charge is *manslaughter*.

See chapter 2 page 15

nominal damages If a judge in a *civil case* considers that the claimant has not suffered any real loss, then he or she may award a very small amount of damages, as a token.

non compos mentis Latin for 'not of sound mind'.

nuisance A form of *tort* or *crime* in which someone interferes with another person's life. For example if you live next door to me in a residential area and set up a workshop in your garden and then use noisy machinery in the middle of the night, I can reasonably complain that you are interfering with my enjoyment of my property, part of which is the assumption that at night it will be peaceful enough for me to get a decent night's sleep. Common forms of nuisance are noise, smells, and air pollution. There are two types of nuisance, *private nuisance* and *public nuisance*. Private nuisance is a tort and public nuisance is a crime.

See chapter 2 page 16

oath Before a witness gives evidence in court (or before someone swears an *affidavit*), they are required to promise solemnly that they will tell the truth. Traditionally this has taken the form of a religious oath: 'I swear by Almighty God that the evidence which I shall give shall be the truth, the whole truth, and nothing but the truth.' Those who object to the religious nature of this wording can opt instead to *affirm*.

offensive weapon It is a criminal offence to be found in possession of an offensive weapon. If you commit *burglary* carrying an offensive weapon, then the more serious charge of aggravated burglary applies. The definition of an offensive weapon is broad. It refers to objects that can cause personal injury and there are three categories: those that are made to cause personal injury, like guns; those that are adapted to cause injury, such as a broken bottle; and those that are intended to cause injury, which could be almost anything.

See chapter 2 page 18

offer An essential part of a *contract* in civil law. One party says in effect, 'If you accept this offer, I will do X.' This must be seriously intended and can be in speech, writing, or through some kind of action.

See chapter 8 page 85

offer to treat Placing goods in a shop window with a price tag on them does not mean that the shopkeeper is obliged to sell them for that price; it is simply an 'offer to treat'. The shopkeeper is saying to the customer, 'I will sell this item if we can agree a satisfactory price.'

Office of Fair Trading The body that regulates trading and protects consumer interests. It can prosecute offending traders in the Restrictive Practices Court, and makes recommendations to the government for changes to the laws governing buying and selling goods.

See chapter 3 page 35

ombudsman An official appointed to investigate complaints in a particular industry or area of public administration. Among others there are ombudsmen for central government, local government, the health service, and the police.

See chapter 7 page 74

ordinary misconduct Behaviour at work that constitutes a disciplinary offence but not one so serious as to lead to instant dismissal (see *gross misconduct*). It would normally lead to discplinary proceedings and, if repeated, might lead to dismissal.

out-of-court settlement See *settlement out of court.*

PACE See *Police and Criminal Evidence Act.*

parental responsibility At the centre of the law relating to children is the concept of responsibility. Whatever the family circumstances into which a child is born, someone assumes a range of duties and powers which the law refers to as parental responsibility. It includes caring for the child's physical needs (food, health, and shelter), and its education. If the child's parents are married, then both parents have parental responsibility and retain it, even if they later divorce. If the parents are unmarried, then the mother alone has parental responsibility and the father only has it if he and the mother sign an agreement to this effect, or if a court orders it.

See chapter 4 page 40

Parliament The *legislature* of England and Wales: the House of Commons and the House of Lords under the Queen. Parliament is regarded as sovereign, which means that there is no higher power. This is not, however, strictly true since in certain areas European Union law is superior to that of Parliament.

See chapter 3 page 21

Parliamentary Commissioner for Administration The Parliamentary *ombudsman* who deals with complaints about wrongful acts by central government departments. Cases are referred to the ombudsman by MPs on behalf of constituents or others.

See chapter 3 page 35

parole French for 'word'. In the past prisoners were sometimes given temporary release if they gave their word that they would return at a certain time. 'Parole' is now used to describe a system of early release of prisoners. After prisoners have served a proportion of their sentences they become eligible for parole. For shorter sentences (up to four years) the proportion is half. Above that it is either half or two thirds. Each case goes before the Parole Board which decides on the basis of reports from the prison and sometimes an interview with the prisoner. Prisoners who commit another crime while on parole may have to serve the rest of their original sentence and may find it harder to get parole next time.

partnership A business arrangement, recognized in the law, between two or more people working together. Each takes a share of the business profits. All are responsible for the conduct of the business and for its debts.

See chapter 2 pages 17–20

penalty clause Sometimes a *contract* will specify the amount of damages to be paid if one party *breaches* the contract, in order to avoid lengthy and expensive litigation. These 'liquidated damages' should reflect the likely amount of financial loss. If they are much higher and are put into the contract to punish the defaulter, this is known as a penalty clause. Courts will not enforce penalty clauses, limiting damages to the amount actually lost.

See chapter 2 page 20

performance One of the ways in which a *contract* can be *discharged*: both parties do what they have agreed to in the contract.

perjury If you are a witness in a trial and deliberately lie under *oath*, you are guilty of perjury. The law takes this very seriously, since if witnesses don't tell the truth, the whole system of legal trials falls apart. Perjury is punishable by a fine and/or up to seven years' imprisonment.

personal property All a person's property except for land and buildings.

personalty *Personal property*.

plaintiff The older term for *claimant*.

plea bargaining In a criminal trial, an agreement between the prosecution and the defence that if the defence will change the plea from not guilty to guilty the prosecution will do something to help the defence (e.g. drop another charge). Sometimes the judge lets it be known that if the plea is changed in this way the sentence will be reduced.

Police and Criminal Evidence Act 1984 The Act of Parliament which governs how the police should behave when questioning, cautioning, and arresting suspects. It also covers how prisoners should be treated and how interviews are to be conducted.

Police Complaints Authority The body that deals with serious complaints against the police. It is sometimes criticized because although it is independent, it does not have independent investigative powers.

police powers of arrest Traditionally the police applied to a magistrate for a warrant before making an arrest. Although this is still possible, they now have wide powers of arrest without the need for a warrant. If they find a person committing an arrestable offence, or believe that they have done so, they can arrest them. Arrestable offences are those which carry a fixed sentence (e.g. murder), or carry a maximum sentence of five years' imprisonment or more, or have been made arrestable offences by Parliament. There are a number of other situations in which the police can arrest people without a warrant, including breach of the peace, driving while disqualified, and disorderly conduct.

See chapter 9 page 90

precedent The principle by which *case law* works is that the judge trying a civil case looks to see whether there has been a case in the past which contains the same features. This provides a precedent for the judgment. If no precedent exists then the judge must interpret cases that are similar and, possibly, create a new precedent.

See chapter 3 page 22

pre-sentence report When a defendant is found guilty the magistrate or judge can consult a report by the probation service before sentencing them. This pre-sentence report will contain background information about the offender—family circumstances and so on. It enables the court to decide, for example, whether a community-based sentence would be suitable.

private law Civil law, the law which covers disputes between individuals or groups of individuals. Its main branches are *tort, contract, family law, company law*.

private nuisance A tort in which someone interferes with the life of another and prevents them from enjoying their property. For example a next-door neighbour may cause

See chapter 2 page 16

excessive noise, or smells. The person affected can take legal action against the offender to gain *damages* or get an *injunction* to stop the action(s). They also have a limited right to seek an *abatement of nuisance*. You can only do this if you have rights (as owner or leaseholder, for example) over the property to which the nuisance is being caused.

private prosecution If the police decide not to prosecute in a criminal case, it is open to private individuals and organizations to do so.

probate Before the *executors* of a will can carry out the dead person's wishes and distribute their *estate* according to the wishes expressed in their will, they have to apply for a certificate from the court. Only when this has been done and probate has been granted can they go ahead. Before probate is granted, the executors or their representatives have to complete forms setting out in detail among other things: the contents of the estate, with valuations of non-monetary items, amounts owed to and by the person who has died, and tax liability.

probation order See *community rehabilitation order*.

See chapter 4 page 46

prohibited steps order One of the orders a court can make in a divorce case controlling the future of the children: it stops one of the parents from specified actions.

prosecution When someone is charged with a crime, the case is heard in court. The English system is 'adversarial', a verbal 'battle' between two sides: the prosecution argues that the *defendant* is guilty, while the defence attempts to prove that this is not the case.

provisional damages In a case involving personal injuries it may be that at the time the court awards damages it is not clear how the injury may affect the claimant mentally or physically in the future. If so, the court can set a figure for damages and tell the claimant that within a certain period they may return to court to have the damages reassessed.

provocation In certain circumstances a defendant in a criminal case can use the defence that someone they attacked provoked them to do it. The court has to decide whether a reasonable person in similar circumstances would have behaved in the same way.

public law As opposed to *private law*, those branches of the law relating to government and administration, and the relationship between the individual and the state. It includes constitutional law and criminal law.

public nuisance A form of *nuisance* which affects more than one person. For example your local shopping centre may be next to an area that is being redeveloped. The building work causes excessive dust which constantly drifts across the shopping area making it unpleasant to use the shops, and even dangerous to the health of those with respiratory problems. Although shoppers have no property rights (so they cannot take action for *private nuisance*) their lives are being interfered with, and a nuisance is being committed. There are three remedies: the firm can be prosecuted (like any other criminal); the local authority can apply for an *injunction* to stop the nuisance; if there is one person who has been more seriously affected than any other (e.g. an asthma sufferer who has had to spend time in hospital as a result of the pollution) they can sue for damages.

See chapter 2 page 16

public order offences The right to demonstrate is limited by the Public Order Act, which makes it an offence to act in such a way as to make a reasonable person fear for their own safety. It defines three offences: *affray, violent disorder,* and *riot.*

See chapter 9 page 96

punitive damages *Exemplary damages.*

qualified privilege A defence against a case of defamation. The defendant argues that the statement complained of was made out of a legal or moral duty. See also *absolute privilege.*

See chapter 9 page 95

Queen's Bench Division The division of the *High Court* that deals with larger cases concerning *tort* and *contract law*. It also deals with requests for *judicial review*.

See note on page 30

Queen's Counsel *Barristers* with at least ten years' experience are eligible for appointment by the *Lord Chancellor* as Queen's Counsels (QCs). They wear a silk gown, so are often referred to as silks. More senior judges are recruited from among the silks.

real property The land (and buildings) that a person owns (not leasehold).

realty *Real property.*

reasonable An important concept in some areas of the law, incorporated in such terms as 'reasonable force', and 'reasonable doubt'. In cases of *tort*, one test is to compare the actions of the defendant with what a reasonable person might have done. If a reasonable person would have behaved with more care, for example, then the defendant has acted negligently. In the past a popular definition of a reasonable person was 'the man on the Clapham omnibus'.

recklessness When someone does something which results in damage or injury, it may be accidental, deliberate, or the result of their negligence. If it is deliberate, then they meant the damage or injury to happen; if it is negligent they didn't mean it to happen but weren't careful enough to stop it happening. If it wasn't deliberate but they knew it could happen but didn't care, then that is recklessness. In cases of criminal damage, a court may also decide it is recklessness if a reasonable person would have realized the damage would happen—even if the defendant didn't realize it.

recorder A part-time judge who takes the least serious cases in the *Crown Court* and, occasionally, cases in the *County Court*. Recorders are appointed from solicitors and barristers with at least ten years' experience.

rectification Putting right unintended errors in a legal document. Documents such as contracts and conveyances can be rectified by applying to a court. If the document doesn't affect anyone else except the parties to it, then they can agree to rectify it without applying to the court.

redundancy One of the grounds on which an employee may be dismissed by an employer. If circumstances have changed since the employee was taken on so that the work they do is no longer needed, the post (not the person) becomes redundant and the person filling it is dismissed.

See chapter 7 page 75

regulation European Union law which is binding on member states.

remand in custody If someone is arrested for a criminal offence they are charged by the police. After that they may be released on police *bail*, or, if the police consider that it is not safe for them to be freed, they are remanded in custody (kept in prison). This decision is made by the *magistrates*.

remand on bail See *bail*.

rescission The cancelling of a *contract* that has become *voidable*.

See chapter 2 pages 17–20

residence order One of the orders that a court may make in a divorce case governing the future of the child(ren). It determines where the child(ren) should live.

See chapter 4 page 46

residuary beneficiary In many wills a number of bequests of specific items or amounts of money are made to individuals, and then whatever remains (the residue) is left to one or more people. They are the residuary beneficiaries.

residue See *residuary beneficiary*.

restraint of trade Part of a contract may limit what one of the parties may do outside the arrangements contained in the contract. For example a recording contract may require a performer to agree not to record for any other company for a fixed period. Such requirements are said to be in restraint of trade because they interfere with the party's ability to trade in the normal way. Courts will only uphold such clauses if they are reasonable and not against the interests of society as a whole.

restrictive covenant A limitation on what a purchaser may do with land he/she has acquired. For example, when you buy a

See chapter 5 page 52

house, you may find that there is a restrictive covenant forbidding the erection of a garden shed larger than a certain size.

See chapter 9 page 91

right of silence A traditional part of English justice used to be that an accused person had the right to remain silent when questioned by the police. The law now says that you may remain silent but that any refusal to answer police questions will be reported at the trial and the jury can interpret it in whatever way they think fit. The *caution* used by the police now contains the words: 'You do not have to say anything. But it may harm your defence if you do not mention when questioned something which you later rely on in court.'

right of audience The right of a barrister (or, in some courts, a solicitor) to plead a case in court.

See chapter 9 page 96

riot An offence under the Public Order Act 1986 committed by twelve or more people acting together to cause 'unlawful violence' towards other people or behaviour such as 'to cause a person of reasonable firmness present at the scene to fear for their personal safety'.

robbery The difference between robbery and *theft* is that if you use violence, or threaten to use violence against someone when stealing something, the offence is robbery, not just theft.

See chapter 3 page 21

Royal Assent When a *bill* has gone through all its stages in *Parliament*, it has to be approved by the Queen ('receive the Royal Assent') before it becomes an Act and the law of the land.

See chapter 8 page 83

satisfactory quality The phrase which is used in recent sale of goods laws to describe goods that are acceptable. Goods which are sold must be accurately described, fit for their purpose, and of satisfactory quality. It means that they must be what a reasonable person would consider satisfactory. This takes into account, among other things, appearance, price, durability, and safety.

self-defence A defence against criminal charges such as assault and battery, manslaughter, and murder: the defendant used reasonable force to protect himself/herself, or family against attack. The court has to decide whether the threat was real (or reasonably believed to be real) and whether the force used was reasonable. If the defendant in a murder trial uses this defence and is found to have used excessive force, then the defence will be rejected.

serious arrestable offences A group of *arrestable offences* including murder, rape, and arson. The police have greater powers when investigating these and can request a longer period in which to interrogate suspects (up to ninety-six hours, instead of twenty-four).

settlement out of court In a *civil case* the claimant and the defendant may decide that they don't want to go through the time and expense of a court case. Instead they agree to settle their differences privately. For example if A has accused B of breaking a contract, B may agree to pay a sum of money in settlement of the case and both then agree that the contract is *voidable*. An out-of-court settlement can be reached at any point before or during a trial up until the judgment.

shorthold tenancy See *assured shorthold tenancy*.

sine die Latin for 'without date'. A court case may be *adjourned* sine die—without a date being set for its resumption.

slander Form of *defamation* that is less serious than *libel* because it is less permanent. Slander is normally spoken and in real time: in other words it leaves no permanent reminder and only lingers in the minds of those who hear it. By contrast libel is in a more permanent form (for example a book or recording) and can be seen or heard at a later date.

See chapter 9 page 94

small claims procedure Claims in a *civil case* for less than £5,000 can be heard by a less expensive and faster method than those in which larger sums of money are involved. Small claims cases are usually heard by a *district judge*.

solicitor A qualified lawyer providing advice and legal services on all aspects of the law. Solicitors have usually spent three years at university leading to a law degree (or a university degree in another subject followed by a year's 'conversion course'), plus a year's legal practice course, leading to an examination. After that they spend a further period employed under a training contract before becoming fully qualified solicitors. At the time of writing there are approximately 85,000 practising solicitors in England and Wales. In the past they could not act as advocates, but now they can do so, working independently or with a barrister. They may still not, however, appear in the higher courts. Many solicitors used to regard themselves as generalists, providing advice and services over the whole range of legal problems faced by clients. Increasingly today they specialize in one or more aspects of the law. This is particularly the case in large companies and partnerships, where clients will be directed to the solicitor specializing in the field that is relevant to their needs.

Solicitor General Deputy to the *Attorney General.*

specific intent crime For some crimes the prosecution has to prove that the defendant intended to commit that particular crime. An example of this is murder, where it is necessary to show that the defendant intended to kill the victim, or at least to cause them serious injury and that death resulted. For other crimes this is not necessary—for example causing death by dangerous driving.

See chapter 4 page 46

specific issue order One of the orders that a court may make in a divorce case governing the future of the child(ren). It makes particular arrangements and is used when the other possible orders are not appropriate.

See chapter 2 pages 17–20

specific performance A court order telling one of the parties to a contract to do what they have agreed to do. For example I may have a contract with you to sell you my stamp collection for a fixed price within a given period. I then discover that one stamp in it is worth a lot more money than I had thought, and will be worth even more in the future. I may prefer to break the contract and pay damages to you, but the court may order that I hand over the stamps for the agreed sum.

standard form contract Contracts are an agreement between two parties, often the result of careful negotiations between the two. Many large companies make use of standard printed contracts which are presented as non-negotiable: the other party can take them or leave them. An example is the 'small print' on the back of hire purchase agreements. Sometimes if you want the goods or services provided you have no choice but to accept. There are, however, limitations on such standard form contracts, notably legislation which stops contracts limiting liability unreasonably, or including terms and conditions which are unfair. Also some contracts which are apparently fixed and standard may, in fact, be negotiable.

See chapter 2 pages 17–20

statement of arrangements In a divorce case the husband and wife have to try to agree what arrangements they are going to make for their child(ren). These are set out in the statement of arrangements.

See chapter 4 page 45

statute law Law that is enacted by the legislature, Acts of Parliament.

statutory instrument A regulation made by a government minister under enabling legislation. Parliament passes a law saying that the minister can make such regulations. This is an example of *delegated legislation*.

strict liability In criminal law this means offences where the prosecution do not have to show *mens rea* (guilty intent). Motoring offences such as speeding come into this category.

subpoena The old name for *witness summons*.

summary offence A criminal offence that must be tried in a Magistrates' Court. Summary offences are the least serious charges. See *triable either way offence* and *indictable offence*.

suspended prison sentence Instead of sending an offender to prison, a court may give a suspended sentence. This means that, provided they do not offend again within a fixed period, they will not have to go to prison, but that if they do they will have to serve the sentence.

See chapter 5 page 51

tenancy in common One of two ways in which two or more people can own a freehold property together, the other being *joint tenancy*. A tenancy in common is one where when one of the owners dies their share of the property becomes part of their *estate* and is distributed in accordance with their *will*.

See chapter 2 pages 17–20

term (of a contract) Part of a contract in which one of the parties promises to do something, makes a statement of fact, or requires the other party to do something. For example A and B might enter into a contract which says that:

(1) A will clean the windows of B's house once a week for 52 weeks.
(2) There are 20 windows in B's house.
(3) B will make 12 monthly payments of £50 to A.

Each of 1-3 is a term of the contract.

testament *Will.*

testator (testatrix) Person making a *will*. *Testator* is masculine, *testatrix* feminine.

testimony Evidence.

theft Taking something that belongs to someone else and intending to keep it and use it as if you were the owner. Even if the rightful owner lent you the goods, it is still theft if you then hang on to them and treat them as your own—for example by trying to sell them as yours. See also *burglary*.

time is of the essence An expression used in contracts where one party (A) requires the other (B) to do something by a certain date. If B fails to do so, then B is in *breach of contract*.

title Right of ownership. 'Good title' means that you can prove it. So, for example, in the case of a house, 'good title' means that you have the deeds or that your ownership is registered with the *Land Registry*.

tort The legal term *tort* comes from a medieval French word meaning 'wrong' or 'injustice'. It is a principle of the legal system that people have a right to security of their persons and property. If that right is infringed, then they are entitled to compensation. (Indeed, if they believe that their rights are about to be infringed they have the right to try to stop it happening.) Another principle is that if by my actions I injure another person or their property then they have the right to claim compensation from me. The commonest forms of tort are: *negligence, defamation, trespass,* and *nuisance.*

See chapter 2 pages 14–16

trade description The description that someone gives when they are selling something. Under the Trade Descriptions Act it is against the law falsely to describe goods that are being sold. If it can be proved that this has been done, then the offender can be required to pay compensation.

See chapter 8 page 85

trespass The word 'trespass' comes from an Old French word meaning *passing across, passage.* A useful substitute word for its legal meaning might be 'interference'. In English law it comes in three forms:

- **trespass to land**: if you pass across a person's land without their permission;
- **trespass to goods**: if you remove a person's property without permission or if you damage it;
- **trespass to person**: if you injure a person physically (*battery*) or make them fear such injury (*assault*), or restrict their freedom of movement (*false imprisonment*).

In all these situations you can sue for damages.

See chapter 2 page 16

triable either way offence A case that can be heard either in a *Magistrates' Court* or in a *Crown Court.*

tribunal Sometimes it is more effective for legal disputes to be resolved outside the framework of the courts, where progress is often slow and expensive. One way in which this is done is by the use of tribunals, hearings at which specialized cases are heard by a panel drawn from lawyers, experts, and lay people. Examples include *Employment Tribunals*, Social Security Appeals Tribunals, and the Special Commissioners of Income Tax.

See chapter 3 page 34

trust A trust arises when one person owns property (in the sense that they have control of it) but is required by law to use it for the benefit for someone else. One example of this is the *executors* of a will; they have the use of the money and property left by the dead person but they have first to pay off taxes due, mortgages, and so on, and then to distribute to the *beneficiaries*. Another example is when money is given or bequeathed to children; it is common to give it in trust until the children reach maturity. The trustees have to look after the money and do what they can to maintain its value, while at the same time ensuring that it is used for the good of the children.

ultra vires A Latin phrase meaning 'beyond the powers'—of a court or regulatory body, for example.

See chapter 7 page 77

unfair dismissal If an employee feels that an employer has behaved unfairly in dismissing them, especially if they have not gone through the proper procedures, they are entitled to claim unfair dismissal and apply to have their case heard by an Employment Tribunal. If the Tribunal finds for the employee, then they can require the employer to reinstate them or, failing that, to compensate them.

See chapter 8 page 86

unfair terms The Unfair Contract Terms Act 1977 says that, among other things, the 'small print' in a contract cannot take away rights that the consumer has under the Sale of Goods Act. These rights were enhanced in 1999 by the Unfair Terms in Consumer Contracts Regulations.

unfit to plead If a defendant in a criminal case is suffering from a mental disability that means that they cannot be tried for the offence, they are judged to be unfit to plead. In this situation they must then be detained in a mental hospital.

vicarious liability If someone working for an employer and carrying out their instructions commits an act which results in an action for *tort* (e.g. *negligence*), then the employer is the one to be sued, not the employee. This is known as vicarious liability.

violent disorder An offence under the Public Order Act 1986. It occurs when three or more people act together to cause 'unlawful violence' towards other people or behaviour such as 'to cause a person of reasonable firmness present at the scene to fear for their personal safety'. If more than eleven people are involved, then the offence becomes *riot*.

See chapter 9 page 96

voidable contract If you enter into a contract with someone who has in fact acted wrongly, the contract is said to be voidable. A contract is voidable if one of these things happens:

- the other party deliberately misled you;
- you were forced into it;
- you were persuaded into it by someone because of their expertise or position and they turned out to be untrustworthy;
- both you and the other party were genuinely mistaken about an important fact which later turned out to be untrue.

If a contract is voidable then the innocent party doesn't have to carry out their side of it, but if they wish they can *affirm the contract*, and continue with its provisions.

See chapter 2 pages 17–20

warrant of arrest If the police want to arrest someone suspected of a crime they can apply to a *magistrate* for a warrant. They have to give the magistrate written evidence and state on oath that in their opinion the person concerned has either committed a crime or is going to commit one. This is less common than it used to be because the police now have very wide powers of arrest that do not require a warrant. (See *arrestable offence*.)

See chapter 9 page 90

will A legal document which explains who is to inherit what when someone dies.

witness summons An order to a witness to attend court to give evidence. It used to be referred to as a subpoena.

wrongful dismissal An employee is wrongfully dismissed if the employer fails to carry out the terms of their contract, typically by failing to give the specified period of notice or payment in lieu.

See chapter 7 page 77

Resources

Organizations

Citizens' Advice Bureau
Offers free advice relating to basic issues such as debt, the family, the workplace, and housing. The nearest office can be found in the phone book. They also have a web site: www.adviceguide.org.uk.

Commission for Racial Equality
A publicly funded, non-governmental body set up under the Race Relations Act 1976 to tackle racial discrimination and promote racial equality. They have a network of regional offices offering information and advice.
St Dunstan's House, 201-211 Borough High Street,
London SE1 1GZ
Telephone: 020 7939 0000
Web site: www.cre.gov.uk.

Disability Rights Commission
An independent body set up by the Government to help secure civil rights for disabled people.
DRC Helpline, Freepost MID 02164, Stratford-upon-Avon
CV37 9HY
Telephone: 08457 622 633
Web site: www.drc-gb.org.

Equal Opportunities Commission
The leading agency working to eliminate sex discrimination in Britain.
Arndale House, Arndale Centre, Manchester M4 3EQ
Enquiry line: 0845 601 5901
Web site: www.eoc.org.uk.

Liberty
Organization campaigning for civil rights.
21 Tabard Street, London SE1 4LA
Advice line: 020 7378 8659
Advice web site: www.YourRights.org.uk.

National Council for One Parent Families
Information for people bringing up children on their own.
255, Kentish Town Road, London NW5 2LX
Lone parent helpline: 0800 018 5026
Web site: www.oneparentfamilies.org.uk.

Solicitors' Family Law Association
An association of over 5,000 solicitors who are committed to promoting a non-confrontational atmosphere in which family law matters are dealt with in a sensitive, constructive, and cost-effective way.
PO Box 302, Orpington, Kent BR6 8QX
Telephone: 01689 850227
Web site: www.sfla.org.uk.

Web sites

All web sites active at the time of publication.

www.acas.org.uk
The Advisory, Conciliation, and Arbitration Service web site, with information about a wide range of employment law issues for both employees and employers.

www.adviceguide.org.uk
The online advice site of the Citizens' Advice Bureaux. A mass of detailed advice under four main headings: 'Your Money', 'Your Family', 'Your Daily Life', and 'Your Rights'. You can browse through areas that interest you, or you can use the search engine provided.

www.cjsonline.org.uk
The Criminal Justice System online. Guidance and downloadable material for victims of crime, people called as witnesses or jurors, and defendants. The site also has detailed guidance on what is involved in being a juror in virtual reality and text forms. (You can even choose the Crown Court you would like to visit!)

www.courtservice.gov.uk
The official site of the UK Court Service. Useful source of official forms and general guidance leaflets on topics such as

divorce, and small claims, all of which can be downloaded in pdf format.

www.cre.gov.uk
The Commission for Racial Equality. Information and guidance on what to do if you are the victim of racial discrimination.

www.drc-gb.org
The Disability Rights Commission. Information and advice about disability issues.

www.employmenttribunals.gov.uk
Information about the work of employment tribunals and advice on attending one, whether as an employer or an employee.

www.eoc.org.uk
The Equal Opportunities Commission. Information and advice about sexual discrimination in the workplace.

www.family-solicitors.co.uk
A site providing access to local solicitors dealing with family matters plus guidance screens on a range of topics from adoption to wills.

www.justask.org.uk
Web site of the Community Legal Service, the government service offering guidance on where to get legal advice and the source of legal aid in civil cases. It offers a number of useful leaflets produced by the Consumers' Association on topics such as divorce, making a will, employment law, renting and letting property, and buying and selling a house.

www.lawcentres.org.uk
Useful information about the work of law centres and the location of the nearest one to you.

www.lawontheweb.co.uk
Interesting and informative 'private enterprise' site, set up by a solicitor, Martin Davies. A huge range of material including 'legal basics' advice on everyday law matters such as road traffic law, family law, and employment law.

www.oneparentfamilies.org.uk
Access to advice for lone parents from the National Council for One Parent Families. Topics include: work; education and training; money matters; children; and splitting up. Some material is available online. There are also leaflets which can be ordered and which are free to lone parents.

www.sfla.org.uk
The site of the Solicitors' Family Law Association. It provides information on where to find a solicitor specializing in non-confrontation family law (just key in your postcode and it comes up with a list). Also a series of online leaflets—screens of text information about family-related topics.

www.tiger.gov.uk
Site managed by the Department of Trade and Industry with very good information about employment law, including downloadable leaflets.

www.YourRights.org.uk
Extensive information and advice about human rights from Liberty, with links to other related organizations. (They also have a web site covering the work of Liberty: www.liberty-human-rights.org.uk.)

BBC sites

The BBC's massive web site (www.bbc.co.uk) contains a variety of legal information under different headings:

www.bbc.co.uk/radio1/onelife/legal/index.htm
This page is the way in to a range of material on the law as it affects everyday life.

www.bbc.co.uk/crime
This provides information from the perspective of a victim or potential victim.

www.bbc.co.uk/watchdog/guides_to
This has simple guides to topics such as buying and renting property, consumer law, employment law, gardening law, and going to court.

Books

General

The New Penguin Guide to the Law
Editor: John Pritchard (Penguin Books)
Very comprehensive (800+ pages) covering the family, housing, welfare benefits, employment, the consumer, insolvency, business, motoring, personal injury, civil liberties, the English legal system.

Law Without a Lawyer
Author: Fenton Bresler (Century)

Wide-ranging, including: birth, maternity rights, marriage, divorce, custody, death, employment, home ownership, motoring.

The Law Machine
Authors: Marcel Berlins and Clare Dyer (Penguin Books)
Highly readable account of the English legal system and the people who work in it.

Oxford Dictionary of Law
Editor: Elizabeth A. Martin (Oxford University Press)
Paperback reference book covering all the legal expressions and concepts you are likely to need and more.

Specific topics

As might be expected, there is a huge variety of titles available. There are, however, two series of books widely available in bookshops and by mail order:

Which?
The Consumers' Association publishes a number of books and self-help kits. These include:

420 Legal Problems Solved
Make Your Own Will
The Which? Guide to Divorce
The Which? Guide to Doing Your Own Conveyancing
The Which? Guide to Getting Married
The Which? Guide to Giving and Inheriting
The Which? Guide to Living Together
The Which? Guide to Renting and Letting
What to Do When Someone Dies
Which? Way to Buy, Own and Sell a Flat
Which? Way to Buy, Sell and Move House
Wills and Probate.

Lawpack publishing
Kits of legal forms:
Last will and testament; Power of Attorney; Residential letting; Limited company; Employment contracts.

Books:
Last will and testament; House buying, selling and conveyancing; Probate; 301 legal forms, letters and agreements; Legal adviser; Personal injury claims; Small claims; Motoring law; Divorce; Cohabitation rights; Home and family solicitor; Legal advice handbook.

Index

Note: **Glossary** definitions are shown in **bold**.